I0120798

# Grow in Concert with Nature

*Sustaining East Asia's Water Resources through Green Water Defense*

*Xiaokai Li, Graeme Turner, and Liping Jiang*

**THE WORLD BANK**
**Washington, DC**

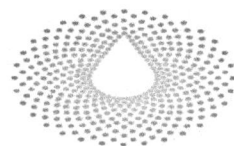

WATER
PARTNERSHIP
PROGRAM

© 2012 International Bank for Reconstruction and Development / The World Bank
1818 H Street NW, Washington DC 20433
Telephone: 202-473-1000; Internet: www.worldbank.org

Some rights reserved

1 2 3 4    15 14 13 12

World Bank Studies are published to communicate the results of the Bank's work to the development community with the least possible delay. The manuscript of this paper therefore has not been prepared in accordance with the procedures appropriate to formally edited texts.

This work is a product of the staff of The World Bank with external contributions. Note that The World Bank does not necessarily own each component of the content included in the work. The World Bank therefore does not warrant that the use of the content contained in the work will not infringe on the rights of third parties. The risk of claims resulting from such infringement rests solely with you.

The findings, interpretations, and conclusions expressed in this work do not necessarily reflect the views of The World Bank, its Board of Executive Directors, or the governments they represent. The World Bank does not guarantee the accuracy of the data included in this work. The boundaries, colors, denominations, and other information shown on any map in this work do not imply any judgment on the part of The World Bank concerning the legal status of any territory or the endorsement or acceptance of such boundaries.

Nothing herein shall constitute or be considered to be a limitation upon or waiver of the privileges and immunities of The World Bank, all of which are specifically reserved.

**Rights and Permissions**

This work is available under the Creative Commons Attribution 3.0 Unported license (CC BY 3.0) http://creativecommons.org/licenses/by/3.0. Under the Creative Commons Attribution license, you are free to copy, distribute, transmit, and adapt this work, including for commercial purposes, under the following conditions:

**Attribution**—Please cite the work as follows: Li, Xiaokai, Graeme Turner, and Liping Jiang. 2012. *Grow in Concert with Nature: Sustaining East Asia's Water Resources through Green Water Defense.* Washington, D.C.: World Bank. DOI: 10.1596/978-0-8213-9588-2. License: Creative Commons Attribution CC BY 3.0

**Translations**—If you create a translation of this work, please add the following disclaimer along with the attribution: *This translation was not created by The World Bank and should not be considered an official World Bank translation. The World Bank shall not be liable for any content or error in this translation.*

All queries on rights and licenses should be addressed to the Office of the Publisher, The World Bank, 1818 H Street NW, Washington, DC 20433, USA; fax: 202-522-2625; e-mail: pubrights@worldbank.org.

ISBN (paper): 978-0-8213-9588-2
ISBN (electronic): 978-0-8213-9597-4
DOI: 10.1596/978-0-8213-9588-2

Cover photo: Dried land near Brisbane, Australia. © iStockphoto, www.istockphoto.com

**Library of Congress Cataloging-in-Publication data has been requested.**

# Contents

## Boxes

## Figures

**Tables**

# Acknowledgments

The report *Grow in Concert with Nature: Sustaining East Asia's Water Resources through Green Water Defense* was prepared by a task team led by Xiaokai Li (Team Leader, Senior Water Resources Management Specialist, EASIN) and comprising Liping Jiang (Senior Irrigation Specialist, EASCS), Paulus Van Hofwegen (Senior Water Resources Specialist, EASIS), Toru Konishi (Senior Economist, EASVS), Weihua Li (Consultant), Tomoko Kato (Operational Analyst, EASIN) and Daniel N. Shemie (TWIWA). The report is based on the Green Water Defense study carried out by the team, with major contributions from Graeme Turner and his colleagues (Department of Sustainability and Environment, Victoria, Australia) and input from Professor Yu Liu (Institute of Water and Hydropower Research, China) for the China case study. This study was conducted under the guidance of John A. Roome (Sector Director, EASSD) and Vijay Jagannathan (Sector Manager, EASIN).

The task team would like to acknowledge the peer reviewers who provided valuable recommendations and comments to this study: Guy Alaerts (Lead Water Specialist, ECSSD), Diego J. Rodríguez (Senior Economist, TWIWA) and Henrike Brecht (Disaster Risk Management Specialist, EASIN). The study also benefited from comments and advice from Julia Bucknall (Sector Manager, TWIWA), Franz R. Drees-Gross (Sector Manager, EASIS), Sudipto Sarkar (Water Practice Leader, EASIN), Paul Kriss (Lead Urban Specialist, EASCS), Paul Procee (Senior Urban Specialist, EASCS), Victor Vergara (Urban Practice Leader, EASIN), Fook Chuan (Senior Water Supply and Sanitation Specialist, EASIS), Ilham Abla (Senior Operation Officer, EASIS) and other colleagues. The team is grateful to Margaret P. Peggy Johnston (Consultant) for her help in editing the report.

Special acknowledgement is due to the Water Partnership Program (WPP) in the World Bank that provided financial support for publishing this report. For more information about the WPP, see http://water.worldbank.org/water/wpp.

# Acronyms and Abbreviations

| | |
|---|---|
| ADB | Asian Development Bank |
| COAG | Council of Australia Government |
| CSIRO | Commonwealth Scientific & Industrial Research Organization |
| DSE | Department of Sustainability and Environment |
| EEA | European Environment Agency |
| ET | Evapo-Transpiration |
| GDP | Gross Domestic Product |
| GEF | Global Environment Facility |
| GL | GigaLiter |
| GMID | Goulburn Murray Irrigation District |
| GRACE | Gravity Recovery and Climate Experiment |
| GWD | Green Water Defense |
| IPCC | Intergovernmental Panel on Climate Change |
| IRBM | Integrated River Basin Management |
| IWEMP | Integrated Water and Environment Management Plan |
| IWMI | International Water Management Institute |
| IWRM | Integrated Water Resources Management |
| JICA | Japan International Cooperation Agency |
| MCM | Million Cubic Meters |
| MDB | Murray-Darling Basin |
| NASA | National Aeronautics and Space Administration |
| NHP | National Hydrological Plan |
| NVIRP | Northern Victoria Irrigation Renewal Project |
| NWC | National Water Commission |
| OECD | Organization for Economic Co-operation and Development |
| PES | Payment for Ecological Service |
| SD | Sustainable Development |
| TWM | Total Water Management |
| UNEP | United Nations Environment Program |
| WUAs | Water User Associations |
| YRCC | Yellow River Conservancy Commission |

# A Summary Note for Policy Makers

## Key Messages

This summary note presents the key concepts and approach of Green Water Defense (GWD) for adaptive water resources (scarcity) management in East Asia. It is intended for policy makers in all East Asia client countries at different institutional levels. The following are key messages about Green Water Defense:

- Green Water Defense is a promising approach of water sector to green growth and sustainable development;
- GWD approach is more cost-effective and sustainable due to its multi-function/benefit orientation;
- GWD requires adaptive management of the spatial layers (ecosystem, infrastructure, and land and water use), key elements (land, water and ecological environment) and their dynamic interactions; GWD endorses participatory spatial planning and management;
- GWD approach calls for a water-resilient and efficient society;
- Water must be managed as a precious resource, a service media and a potential risk factor in different forms, which requires management in its totality (i.e., total water management) during all phases (i.e., water cycle management).
- GWD approach to water resources management is based on the principle of 'living and building with nature' and maximizing water productivity;
- Water development and management should be right-based, productivity focused and oriented towards multiple functions and wins (productive use, conservation and risk reduction);
- GWD approach to water management requires involving stakeholders, combining demand and supply-side management, balancing structural and non-structural measures; and
- Well-conceived incentive policies and market mechanisms are essential to behavior change in water use and risk management and in applying GWD approach.

## Key Challenges for Managing Water Resources in East Asia Region

East Asia is home to more than a quarter of the world's population. It saw impressive economic growth in the past decade, accompanied by rapid population growth and urbanization. As a result, land and water resources in this region are under increasing pressure leading to over-exploitation, use conflicts, and other water insecurity issues. Under a changing climate, such pressure tends to intensify in terms of the area and population affected by water scarcity and insecurity (See Figure E.1). The most compelling water resources management issues in East Asia can be summarized as follows:

- *Increasing water scarcity.* Although most East Asia countries are endowed with plenty of water resources, water scarcity in many regions is becoming more prominent in recent years due to spatial and temporal variability and changing

**Figure E.1:  Projected global water scarcity in 2025**

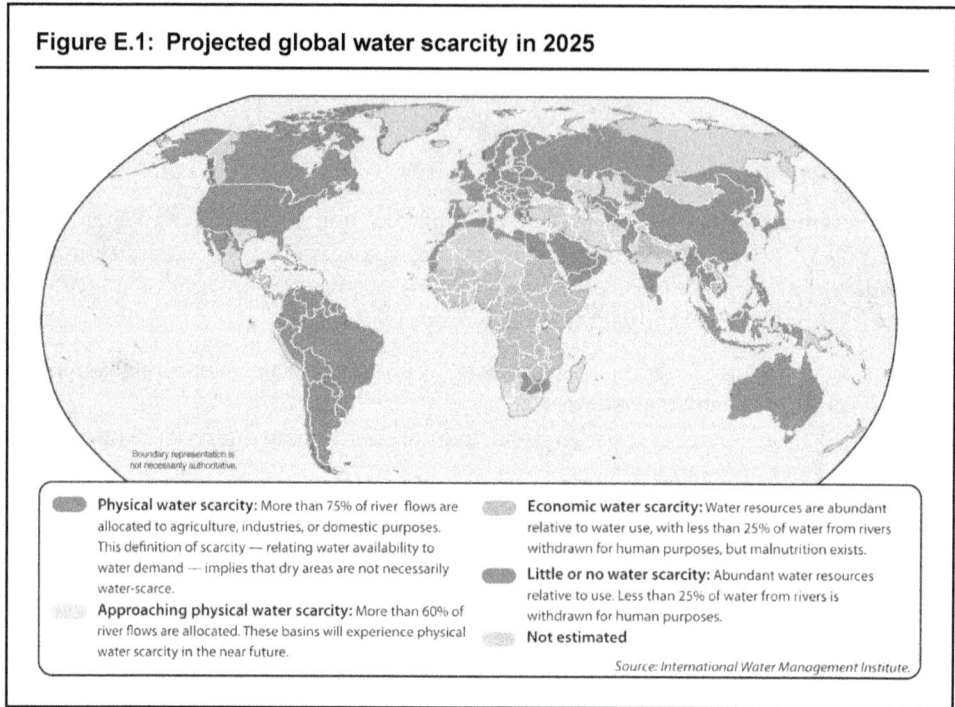

Boundary representation is
not necessarily authoritative.

**Physical water scarcity:** More than 75% of river flows are allocated to agriculture, industries, or domestic purposes. This definition of scarcity — relating water availability to water demand — implies that dry areas are not necessarily water-scarce.

**Approaching physical water scarcity:** More than 60% of river flows are allocated. These basins will experience physical water scarcity in the near future.

**Economic water scarcity:** Water resources are abundant relative to water use, with less than 25% of water from rivers withdrawn for human purposes, but malnutrition exists.

**Little or no water scarcity:** Abundant water resources relative to use. Less than 25% of water from rivers is withdrawn for human purposes.

**Not estimated**

*Source: International Water Management Institute.*

*Source:* International Water Management Institute

climate. For example, the 2010 drought in the Mekong Delta affected more than 1,300ha of rice fields, with enormous economic losses (OECD, 2010);

- *Rising cost of flood damage.* Flood damage caused by such factors as improper land use, extreme weather and sea level rise is more frequent in East Asia, especially in the low lying deltas where many of the large cities (Bangkok, Jakarta, Manila and Ho Chi Minh City, etc) are located, as reflected by the 2011 floods in Thailand and the Philippines;

- *Water pollution and ecosystem degradation.* Many rivers and lakes in the region are heavily polluted, e.g., Hai River in China and rivers in Jakarta area of Indonesia, endangering the biodiversity and proper functioning of these water systems to provide critical water services. This condition is a result of both improper land use (leading to land erosion and sedimentation) and point and non-point source pollution caused by different water users; and

- *Climate change and variability.* Many parts of East Aisa, especially the coastal and low-lying delta regions, are very vulnerable to climate change impact in the form of extreme climate events, storm surge and sea level rise, etc. The climate variability observed in recent years is expected to continue and possibly become more extreme in the coming decades, posing an enormous challenge to water management in the region.

The purpose of the 'Towards Green Water Defense in East Asia' study is to take stock of advances in management practices, institutional and technological innovations for managing water resources under changing climate. The focus of this note is on adaptive management of physical water scarcity.

## Green Water Defense Conceptual Framework and Approach

Green Water Defense is an adaptive management philosophy and approach which seeks to spatially integrate natural forces and artificial interventions, and to balance incentive-based and supply-driven measures, with minimum footprints and externalities in sustainably providing water services and managing related climate risks. It is enlightened by the green growth thinking and builds on a number of other concepts and approaches (see figure E.2), including (a) Live with nature and build with nature; (b) Green adaptation and low impact development; (c) Integrated river basin and coastal zone management; (d) Productivity-based agricultural water management (produce more with less); and (e) Water-sensitive urban design and eco-dynamic design.

*GWD Conceptual Framework*

Conceptually, GWD can be illustrated by a simple spatial model (see figure E.3) that consists of three spatial layers—the Base Layer (representing the ecosystem—air, water and soil), the Network Layer (representing the infrastructure system) and the Occupation Layer (representing the human actions in land & water use), each with different and interrelated temporal dynamics and public-private involvement (VROM 2001). The model indicates a physical hierarchy in which the Base Layer influences the other layers through enabling and constraining factors, similar to the dynamic interactions and connections among economy, society and environment. For instance, the soil type in the Base Layer determines to a large extent the kind of agriculture that can be performed in the Occupation Layer. Unfavorable conditions (constraints) posed by the Base Layer can be mitigated through adaptations in the Network Layer and/or Occupation Layer. The GWD approach seeks to promote dynamic and healthy interactions among the three layers in an integrated manner, to achieve sustainability of the ecosystem, and of water and land use in providing the required services and managing related climate risks.

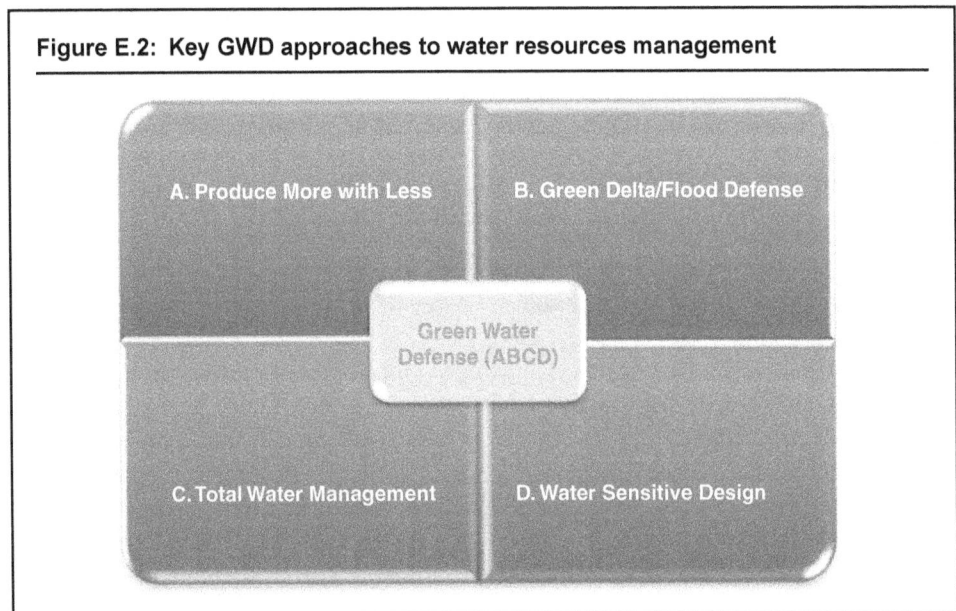

**Figure E.2: Key GWD approaches to water resources management**

A. Produce More with Less

B. Green Delta/Flood Defense

Green Water Defense (ABCD)

C. Total Water Management

D. Water Sensitive Design

*Source:* Authors

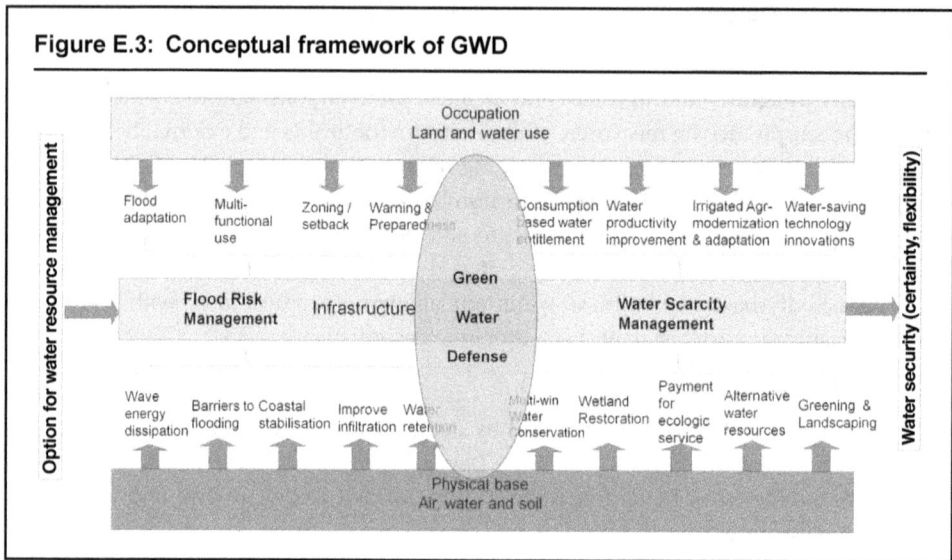

**Figure E.3: Conceptual framework of GWD**

*Source:* Authors

Conventional approaches to water management tend to emphasize the utility of expensive water infrastructures such as dikes and reservoirs for flood control and water supply purposes. The GWD approach makes full use of the ecosystem function (in the forms of natural forces and/or processes), and aims to balance non-structural and structural measures, and promotes land and water uses and infrastructure planning and designs that are cost-effective and enhance ecosystem or at least avoid significant harm to it. For example, water-productivity improvement (in the Occupation Layer) serves to enhance ecosystem (the Base Layer) through water consumption reduction and consequently pollution reduction. Similarly, payment for ecological services (in the Base Layer) encourages people to use water wisely and efficiently (in the Occupation Layer). The three layers linked by the GWD, function as a dynamic system to be capable of achieving water security, certainty and flexibility, as demonstrated in Figure E.3.

*Key Principles of GWD Approach*

The GWD approach adheres to the following basic principles:

(a) It adopts sustainability as the overarching principle in integrated water-land-ecosystem use planning and management, which covers technical, institutional and financial aspects;

(b) It examines issues and solutions from a spatial perspective and in a dynamic manner, supported by modern tools and information technology for robust decision making;

(c) It makes best use of natural forces and processes through ecological services, and maintains healthy dynamics between natural and built environments;

(d) It advocates stakeholder involvement and cross-sectoral collaboration in finding multiple win solutions through alignment with stakeholders' interests;

(e) It seeks to integrate supply and demand-side management measures in adaptive water management;

(f) It endeavors to balance structural and non-structural measures for more sustainable solutions; and

(g) It adheres to the cost-effectiveness criterion for options assessment and measures prioritization and selection, based on the concept of 'buying-down the risks' taking into account the associated social and environment costs and benefits.

### Key Elements of GWD Approach

In designing the GWD management strategy and measures, the key elements to be included are as follows.

**Knowledge Requirements.** The following represents the fundamental knowledge requirement for adaptive water scarcity management:

(a) *Establish current status of inputs and trends.* This includes using climate, ecological and socio-economic data to assess supply limits, environmental flow needs and water use values. Long term climate data and climate projections are also important data requirements;

(b) *Determine water system boundary.* The boundary should be set at definable physical limits such as catchment, aquifer or river basin limits which recognize water flow paths and interconnection of definable water resources. If possible, political or administrative boundaries should have a lesser importance;

(c) *Decide on water availability.* Assessment should be conducted on the available water resources that can be supplied from the water system by modeling the behavior of the water system under a range of climate scenarios;

(d) *Determine sustainable water use requirements.* Investigations should be undertaken to determine ecological values of a water system, their potential services, and their water regime requirements; and

(e) *Assess risks to the resources.* The risks to the resources need to be assessed and factored into allocation decision-making processes.

**Management Tools.** Essential tools required for a GWD approach to water resources (scarcity) management are as follows:

(a) *Water allocation planning.* This involves water accounting, establishing supply reliability requirements, and a priority of supply hierarchy between various users (e.g., towns, agriculture, environment and recreation/society), setting a cap and establishing a trade off process;

(b) *Water entitlement system.* This is the core mechanism for managing water systems where demand is, or has the potential, to be greater than the supply. It is a prerequisite for the establishment of water markets or trading systems to allow reallocation of water efficiently to higher value uses and to facilitate supply efficiency improvement. The implementation of entitlement systems requires accurate measurement of supplies;

(c) *Publicly accessible water registers.* These are required to record entitlements ownership details, total entitlement volume, seasonal allocation allowed against the entitlement. They are important where water allocation has been capped and provide essential information for water managers and the operation of water markets and trading systems;

(d) *Economically viable and efficient infrastructure.* There are many structural solutions to improve the water supply efficiency of supply works. These need to be adapted to the circumstances which involve major expenditure of often limited funds. These works must be accompanied by incentives to ensure the works are maintained and the improved supply efficiencies are retained;

(e) *Demand management and water conservation.* They refer to policy and management interventions to curtail water demand, reduce consumption and protect water and related ecological systems; and

(f) *Augmentation from alternative water sources.* This involves use of recycled water, brackish water, rain/storm water harvesting, etc for portable and non-portable uses, respectively.

## Key GWD Measures from Best Practice Case Studies

While local considerations including socio-economic conditions, determine the specific approach and GWD measures, the following provides a summary of the key GWD measures from the best practice case studies:

- *Water resources management at all levels can benefit enormously from a strong water conservation culture.* Such initiative as 'building a water-conservation society' serves to raise public and water users' awareness of water scarcity and sense of urgency to use water efficiently and increase communities' resilience to climate variability through adapting to uncertain water availability;

- *Managing water scarcity successfully requires a portfolio of measures,* ranging from a clear strategy, strong legal framework (including clear ownership of water), supporting policy and regulations (institutional mechanisms), appropriate economic and financial instruments, technological innovations, and targeted water management investments (e.g., water conservation initiatives by main users and targeted productivity improvement programs). Maintaining a good balance between very limited water resources available and increasing water demand requires strict management of water allocation and distribution system to ensure that it operates at a high level of efficiency for different uses—domestic, industrial and agricultural, as illustrated in the Israeli case. Further, the uncertainty surrounding future conditions means that planning needs to be based on a wide range of plausible future climate scenarios;

- *Improving consumption-based water productivity is at the heart of adaptive water scarcity management.* Improving water productivity is the combined effect of many factors. In Israel, the increase in agricultural water productivity can be attributed to the supportive government policy, advances in irrigation technology, changes in cropping pattern, use of alternative water sources and the skills of farmers and their ability to adopt innovative technologies and best management practices;

- *Effective water scarcity management calls for* establishing a clearly defined and transparent water allocation and entitlement system which allocates water from basin to different levels of governments/water authorities and to water users, and provides for a mechanism of reallocation and transfer/trading, as demonstrated in the Victoria case. Secure entitlements to water and a transparent water trading system are crucial for managing water variability. They provide certainty and clarity regarding responsibility for actions under a range of conditions;

- *Agricultural water use has a large potential in water saving* through a comprehensive package of water-saving measures (technical, management and agricultural measures). This can be realized through targeted water-saving and productivity improvement programs combined with demand-side management mechanisms such as volumetric water pricing and promotion of crop diversification, and WUA-based participatory irrigation management;

- *An ET-based approach to water scarcity management* which targets reduction in consumptive use or ET, can lead to real (agricultural) water savings and effectively results in sustaining water use in physically water-stressed areas. This is in contrast with the conventional irrigation-efficiency focused approach that usually results in increases of water consumption through expansion of effective irrigation areas. The ET-based management approach proved to be effective in the North China Plain for adaptive water scarcity management and water productivity improvement;

- *A comprehensive water conservation practice aligned with farmers' interests* can have multiple-win effects of reducing water consumption and environmental impact and increasing farm incomes. A comprehensive approach, involving not only engineering works upgrading but also irrigation management and agricultural practice improvements, makes possible increasing farm incomes while reducing water consumption and gradually restoring groundwater levels in groundwater irrigated areas. Initiatives of agricultural water saving and productivity improvement are more likely to succeed if they give priority to user/farmer incentives to change water use and management practices;

- *Through addressing the water-energy use linkage,* water utilities can minimize environmental impact and reduce operating costs. The same principle applies to wastewater management and pumping irrigation and drainage;

- *Water right trading as illustrated in the case of Victoria, Australia, is very effective* in reallocating water to high value use and thus in increasing water productivity. Similarly, at a lower scale level, the agriculture-industry water trading pilots in northern China through industry-supported agricultural water saving showed promising results in increasing water productivity and in reducing total water consumption;

- *Virtual water trade cross countries or regions,* as demonstrated by the Spanish case, can be an effective strategy in reducing agricultural water consumption and mitigating water shortage at different scale levels;

- *Coping with water shortage calls for both demand* and *supply-side management measures.* Nonstructural measures such as water conservation and demand management are very cost-effective investments in bridging the supply-demand gaps and enhancing water security. Most significant contributions to reduction in urban water demand are from tariff (structure and level) adjustment and technological innovations in industrial, business and residential uses;

- *Incentive policies and economic instruments* can stimulate and enable different use sectors to engage in rigorous water conservation through diversifying water sources, technological innovations and adoption of best management practices, in irrigated agriculture, and in municipal and industrial water uses; and

▪ *A multi-stakeholder participatory approach is indispensable* for effective urban; and agricultural water management. Stakeholders, such as farmer user groups, urban water corporations and environmental water managers, are generally best placed to manage their own risks under the constraints of their operating environment. Good communication and collaboration among different water management authorities responsible for different aspects of water management and stakeholder groups are essential when dealing with water shortage, pollution and droughts, etc.

## Towards a Roadmap for GWD Application in East Asia

### General Process for Applying GWD Approach

Application of GWD approach in terms of selecting the appropriate GWD measures are very location specific. The following is intended to provide a guide for the general process of strategy formulation, management measures selection and implementation:

▪ *Establish the knowledge base:* This includes water resources accounting and assessment, water register, water management asset inventory, documentation of management institutions, hydro-met monitoring network, water management information system (preferably with spatial database) and a decision-support system;

▪ *Map key issues in relation to the key water services at different scales (basin and national/ local government scales):* The issue identification must be based on a robust analysis of plausible (land and water) development scenarios factoring in likely climate change and variability, and results of institutional analysis and an infrastructure needs assessment;

▪ *Formulate strategies at different scale levels with shared vision and objectives for water allocation and (consumptive) use management:* Use both market mechanism and government regulation with stakeholder (particularly user community) participation;

▪ *Raise the awareness of the water users and general public* of the water (scarcity) issues and nurture a culture of water conservation, through public campaigns and education initiatives;

▪ *Establish effective management organizations* with cross-sectoral coordination mechanism for investment planning and decision making;

▪ *Develop policies and regulations* to promote water-efficient development and water conservation, and stimulate technological and institutional innovations;

▪ *Identify and assess options of key GWD management measures* (structural and non-structural) to address the issues identified at the target level. Different sets of measures can be formulated and screened in light of their contributions and appropriateness for the specific circumstances;

▪ *Prioritize the management measures based on their cost effectiveness:* Cost effectiveness analysis taking into account the social and ecological costs and benefits, is the objective criterion for investment prioritization and selection. Lessons of best practices from the case studies could serve as practical references; and

▪ *Develop and implement action plans based on local endorsements and constraints.* Pilot GWD measures if they involve much uncertainty, before scaling-up or mainstreaming. Targeted government programs, public-private partnership initiatives and water development and management projects, supported by development partners such as the World Bank, Asian Development Bank and bilateral organizations, are good vehicles for piloting and implementing adaptive water management.

### Focus of GWD Approach for Different Spatial Scales

The applicability of the GWD measures depends on the nature and location of the water system, social-economic circumstances, institutional framework and infrastructure network conditions, etc. Furthermore, applying those measures at different scale levels also means different focus. Generally speaking, at the national or a local government level, the high priority should be on creating a policy and institutional framework for water allocation and use management, land use control, and adaptive management financing, as well as on raising public awareness and building a water-sensitive society; at the basin level, the focus needs to be more on establishing a flexible water allocation and entitlement system, multi-stakeholder decision making mechanism, integrated development and management planning, a solid water management information and knowledge base and decision-support tools; at the water system level, total water (or water portfolio) management, alignment with water users' interests, and modernizing the essential infrastructure, deserve high attention. To illustrate the application of GWD approach in managing water scarcity, a practical case in East Asia is presented in Chapter 6.

# CHAPTER 1

# Introduction

## Water Scarcity and Climate Change

As countries develop, the demand for water increases while water supply becomes less certain and is often not enough to meet demand. In general, pressures from both environment and human activities can increase the likelihood of water scarcity. Such pressures include increased socio-economic development and population growth, change in people's diets, competition for available water among different user sectors and growing climate variability.

Climate change is likely to exacerbate the existing demand and supply stresses, particularly when more frequent and extreme droughts and floods, as well as rising sea level are becoming more evident. In temperate, sub-temperate regions, less rainfall and longer dry seasons are expected. In tropical areas, rainfall is predicted to be similar or greater in terms of annual average volumes, more intense and severe storms and seasonal droughts (IPCC, 2007). These pressures will test the effectiveness of water resource management systems in providing a consistent and secure water supply for all users, with minimum externalities.

Water scarcity can occur through reduced supply, poor water quality or restriction of access. It can occur in all climates, including regions with high annual average rainfall. Vietnam, for example, has abundant water available (9,856 m$^3$ per person a year). However, the Dong Nai river Basin in southern Vietnam, one of the most economically significant basins, is classified as highly stressed during the dry season (i.e., June to October). During this period there are severe water shortages that affect rice cropping intensity and result in insufficient rice production to meet the basic demand of the basin's population (NTPSWS 2009). In Australia's largest irrigation basin, the Murray-Darling basin, water is becoming scarce as a result of both reduced supply and poor quality water in the lower reaches. Reduced flows have been a consequence of over-allocation for human uses and an extended dry period. This situation has led to increased salinity levels in the two major lakes at the end of the system where the river meets the ocean. The poor water quality caused by high salinity means that the lakes are no longer reliable for irrigation, feeding livestock or human consumption.

## Objectives of the Study

This study will assess advances in management practices, institutional and technological innovations for managing water scarcity sustainably under a changing climate. The impetus for this analysis comes from the World Bank's concept note 'Towards Green Water Defense (GWD) in East Asia' study, specifically one of the building blocks of the GWD concept: *Managing water scarcity by "producing more with less" or increasing water productivity and reducing undesirable externalities.*

This study of 'Sustaining East Asia's Water Resources through Green Water Defense' is a sub-study of the 'Towards Green Water Defense (GWD) in East Asia' study and is complemented by another sub-study 'Green Water Defense for Flood Risk Management in East Asia' that focuses on flood management in delta regions.

The report has the following specific objectives, reflected in the structure of the report.

- To provide a brief overview of the status of water resources in East Asia, including the diversity of climates, the extent of physical water scarcity and potential changing climate impacts;
- To summarize major management measures being implemented in selected countries where water is, or has the potential to become scarce, and how they fit in the green water defense concept;
- To document key lessons learned from best practices in managing scarce water resources from experiences in the country case studies; and
- To provide a roadmap for East Asian countries to apply the GWD approach in addressing water scarcity issues and improving water security.

The report is written primarily to inform World Bank staff, client country water resource managers and policy makers, water resources specialists and other water professionals engaged in different aspects (e.g., investment planning and management, and operation) of water resources management. It builds on a number of completed studies and analysis, including the World Bank flagship studies related to climate change adaptation and water resources management in East Asia[1].

## Methodology

The case study approach gathers lessons of best practices for managing water resources that have the potential or have already become scarce. The GWD conceptual framework for managing scarce water resources (see Chapter 2) guided this approach. The focus was primarily on experiences in Australia and in other selected countries. The Australian experience draws from an in-depth analysis of the over-allocated Murray-Darling Basin system. These findings were supplemented by lessons drawn from reviews of documented experiences in other drought-vulnerable countries, including Spain, China and Israel.

Reports prepared on the status and practices of water resources management in Victoria, Australia and in northern China provide background information and detailed analysis for this study. The main information sources used to prepare this report are government reports, peer-reviewed literature and discussions with water managers in some of the country case studies.

## Notes

1. See, e.g., *Water Anchor.* World Bank, 2009; *Climate Change Adaptation in Water Resources Management.* World Bank, 2010; *Economics of Climate Change Adaptation.* Asian Development Bank, World Bank, Japan International Cooperation Agency, 2010; *Asian Mega-City Climate Change Impact Assessment.* World Bank, 2008

# CHAPTER 2

# Status of Water Resources in East Asia

## Topography and Climate

East Asia is a vast region consisting of coastal areas, fertile inland plains and large high plateaus and mountain ranges far from the sea. Such a highly varied topography contains a diverse and complex range of climates, as illustrated by the Koeppen-Geiger climate classification, which shows that East Asia includes more than six main climate types (see figure 2.1).

Monsoonal flows are key influences on Asia's climates and lead to extreme variability in seasonal rainfall. The East Asian Monsoon steers the climate of China, the republic of Korea, Vietnam, Laos, Cambodia and the Philippines, and is characterized by warm and wet summers from May to August and cold and dry winters. Indonesia and Malaysia's climate is influenced by the Indo-Australian Monsoon, characterized by a wet season from December to March and a dry season from June to September.

**Figure 2.1: Map of East Asia climates**

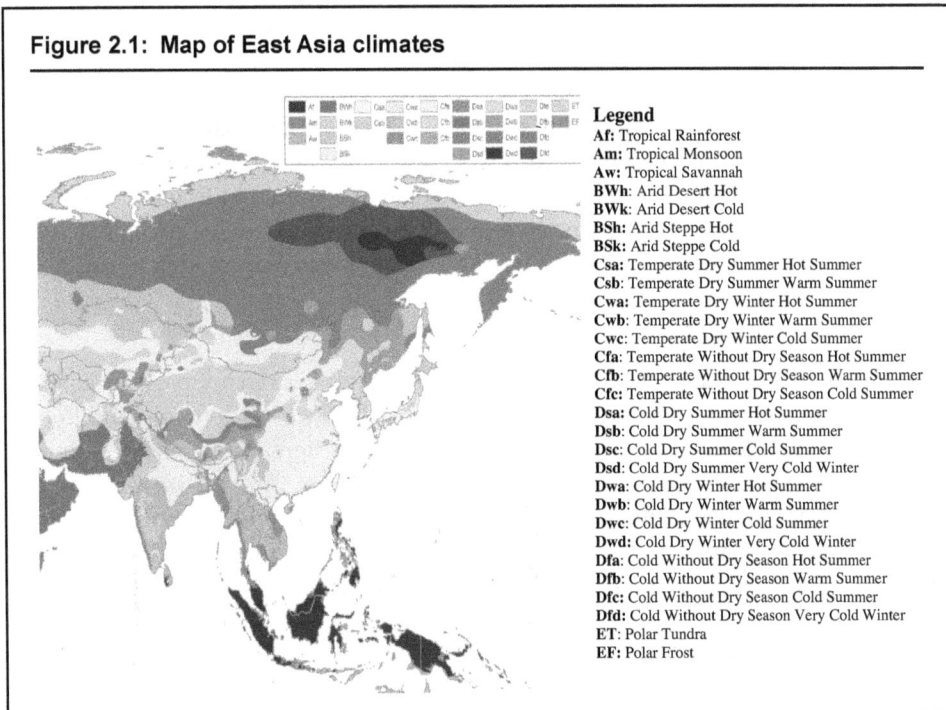

**Legend**
**Af:** Tropical Rainforest
**Am:** Tropical Monsoon
**Aw:** Tropical Savannah
**BWh:** Arid Desert Hot
**BWk:** Arid Desert Cold
**BSh:** Arid Steppe Hot
**BSk:** Arid Steppe Cold
**Csa:** Temperate Dry Summer Hot Summer
**Csb:** Temperate Dry Summer Warm Summer
**Cwa:** Temperate Dry Winter Hot Summer
**Cwb:** Temperate Dry Winter Warm Summer
**Cwc:** Temperate Dry Winter Cold Summer
**Cfa:** Temperate Without Dry Season Hot Summer
**Cfb:** Temperate Without Dry Season Warm Summer
**Cfc:** Temperate Without Dry Season Cold Summer
**Dsa:** Cold Dry Summer Hot Summer
**Dsb:** Cold Dry Summer Warm Summer
**Dsc:** Cold Dry Summer Cold Summer
**Dsd:** Cold Dry Summer Very Cold Winter
**Dwa:** Cold Dry Winter Hot Summer
**Dwb:** Cold Dry Winter Warm Summer
**Dwc:** Cold Dry Winter Cold Summer
**Dwd:** Cold Dry Winter Very Cold Winter
**Dfa:** Cold Without Dry Season Hot Summer
**Dfb:** Cold Without Dry Season Warm Summer
**Dfc:** Cold Without Dry Season Cold Summer
**Dfd:** Cold Without Dry Season Very Cold Winter
**ET**: Polar Tundra
**EF**: Polar Frost

*Source:* Peel et al. 2007, p. 1639.

The low lying eastern and southern regions of China, northern Vietnam and coastal South Korea demonstrate a subtropical climate with hot and humid summers and dry, mild-to-cool winters. Annual average rainfall is relatively low in the north (e.g., approximately 521 mm at Beijing) and can be unreliable during drought periods. In contrast, annual average rainfall is high in southern China and northern Vietnam (1,683 mm at Guangzhou and 1,680 mm at Hanoi), mostly due to summer rainfall generated by the East Asian Monsoon and typhoons. Occasionally, typhoons move further north to affect the central coast of China.

The high plains and deserts of China's northern interior and Mongolia have a cold desert climate, characterized by large temperature differences between summer and winter. Summers are typically hot and winters are cold (Urumqi has a mean maximum temperature of -13°C in January and 25°C in July). The region is located within the rain shadow of a number of significant mountain ranges, which impedes monsoonal rainfall. Annual average rainfall overall in the region is low (about 236 mm at Urumqi).

With elevations above 3,600 meters, the Tibetan Plateau and the Himalayas have a harsh alpine climate, characterized by short, rainy and cool summers and extremely cold, dry winters. Rainfall is influenced by the East Asian Monsoon, and most rain occurs from June to September. Annual average rainfalls are moderately low at around 400 to 450 mm.

Tropical climates dominate the southern countries of East Asia. Southern Vietnam, Thailand, Cambodia, the Lao People's Democratic Republic (Lao PDR), and the eastern Philippines all have tropical wet and dry climates, dominated by the East Asian Monsoon. Annual average rainfall is generally above 1,000 mm across the region, and reaches up to 2,500 mm on seaside facing highlands. Most rainfall occurs between May and October.

Further south in Indonesia and east Malaysia, all seasons are hot and humid, and there is very little seasonal variation in temperature, which ranges between 26 and 31°C. The main variable of this tropical rainforest climate is rainfall, which is controlled by the Indo-Australian Monsoon. Generally speaking, the dry season occurs between May and September and the wet season between November and March. The wettest area in this region records average annual rainfall of more than 2,000 mm. The islands closer to Australia are typically drier, with some areas receiving over 1,000 mm of rainfall per year.

Average seasonal rainfall across the East Asia region is illustrated in figure 2.2.

## Observed Rainfall Trends

There is evidence suggesting that total annual rainfall over many parts of East Asia, e.g., in China, is increasing, as is the frequency of days with heavy rain and flooding (see figure 2.3). Recent studies have found there are signs of increasing rainfall in the Yangtze basin, as well as in northwest and southeast China, with changes up to 30 percent. However, decreases in rainfall have been observed in central China, the Yellow River basin and in northern China. Studies have also found that the strong variation in seasonal rainfall across much of southern and eastern China has also decreased.

## Impacts of Climate Change

While future summer monsoons may bring more rainfall to East Asia, climate change may increase the annual variability of monsoon rainfall.

**Figure 2.2: Average seasonal rainfall across the Asia/Pacific region (1979–1995)**

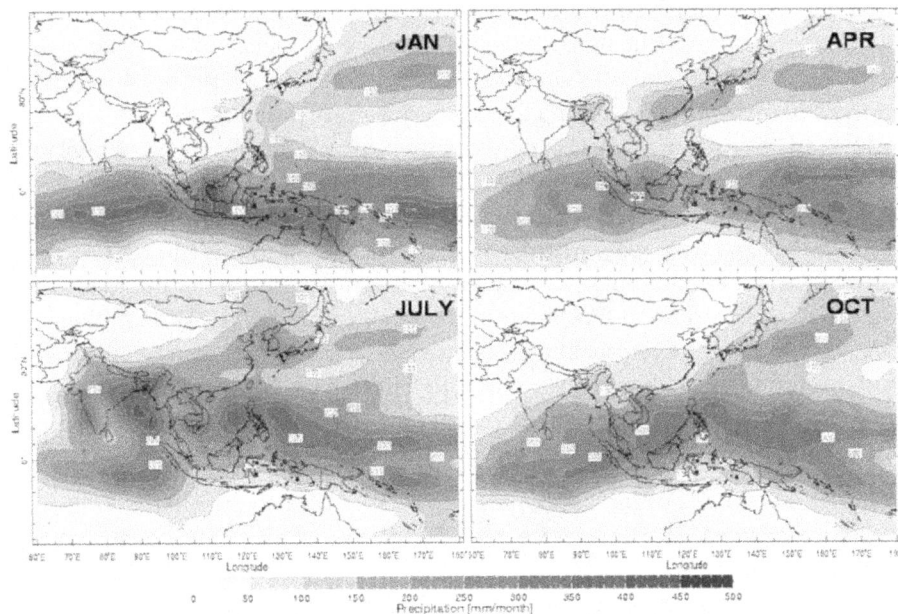

*Source:* Preston et al., 2006.

**Figure 2.3: Change in annual total rainfall for China**

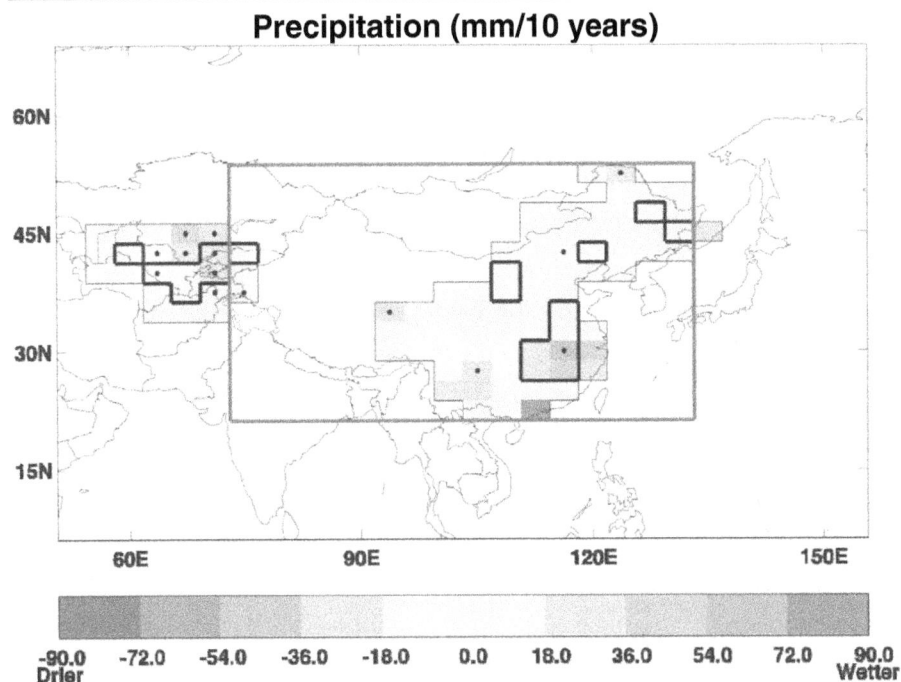

*Source:* UK MetOffice, 2011.

Such variability could restrict any benefits associated with increased average rainfall. Monsoon variability is also tied to the El Niño Southern Oscillation, with drought risk increasing during El Niño events, yet there is little agreement among climate models regarding how future climate change may alter the frequency or intensity of El Niño events (UK Met Office 2011).

In addition, studies examining the effects of aerosol particles (e.g., black carbon and organic carbon from incomplete combustion as well as from dust) on South Asia climate indicate that such aerosols may significantly reduce regional rainfall.

The results of climate change modeling imply a potential for increased rainfall over East Asia, as well as an increase in extreme rainfall events in part of China (see figure 2.4) (UK Met Office 2011). Generally this potential is due to increase in rainfall over the summer monsoon (Preston et al. 2006). According to the UK Met Office (2011) several climate change impact studies have predicted that the trend of increased flood events will continue, although their uncertainties are significant.

## Key Water Resources Management Issues in East Asia

Similar to many parts of the developing world, East Asia countries face multiple challenges in managing their water resources despite the encouraging progress they have made on different fronts. These challenges can be categorized into the following groups of key issues: (a) increasing water scarcity (see the trend in figure 2.5) and use competition, as experienced by most parts of Northern China, Eastern Indonesia and lower Mekong riparians (Laos PDR, Cambodia, Thailand and Vietnam) in recent years; (b) water pollution and deterioration of ecological system as a results of rapidly increasing water withdrawal, lack of treatment facilities and effective pollution control mechanisms-water quality situations in China's major rivers, Jakarta, Mekong Delta and Manila are

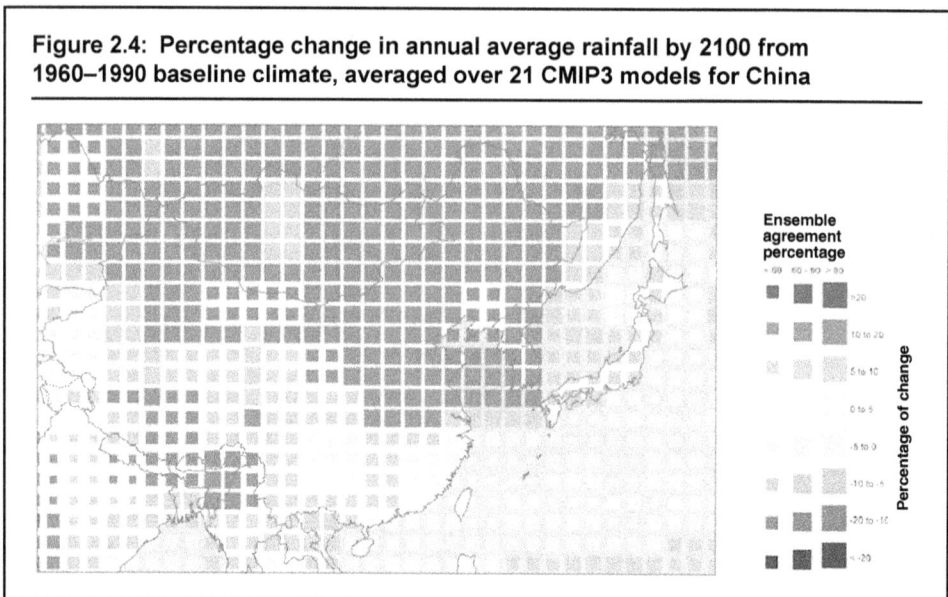

Figure 2.4: Percentage change in annual average rainfall by 2100 from 1960–1990 baseline climate, averaged over 21 CMIP3 models for China

*Source:* UK MetOffice, 2011.

**Figure 2.5: Projected global water scarcity in 2025**

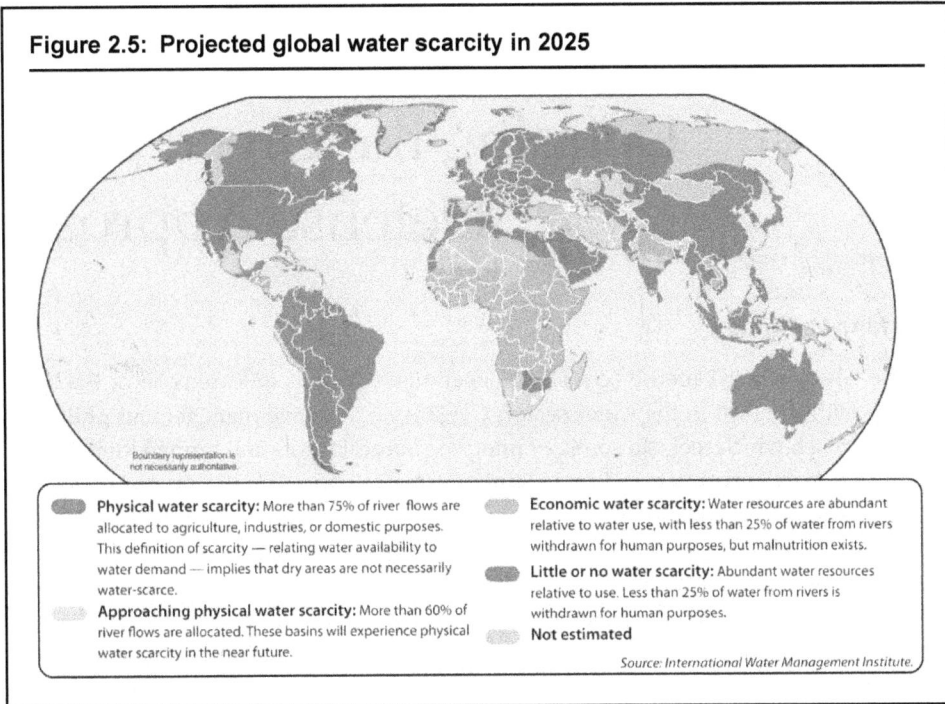

Physical water scarcity: More than 75% of river flows are allocated to agriculture, industries, or domestic purposes. This definition of scarcity — relating water availability to water demand — implies that dry areas are not necessarily water-scarce.

Approaching physical water scarcity: More than 60% of river flows are allocated. These basins will experience physical water scarcity in the near future.

Economic water scarcity: Water resources are abundant relative to water use, with less than 25% of water from rivers withdrawn for human purposes, but malnutrition exists.

Little or no water scarcity: Abundant water resources relative to use. Less than 25% of water from rivers is withdrawn for human purposes.

Not estimated

Source: International Water Management Institute.

*Source:* International Water Management Institute

examples (Millennium Ecosystem Assessment 2005); (c) high level of vulnerability to climate change particularly in deltas and coastal regions; and increasing flood damages in scale and frequency as shown in the dramatic flood disasters in most Southeast Asia nations: Thailand, the Philippines, Vietnam and Indonesia over the past years (World Bank 2011); (d) major gaps in water management information base and infrastructure network which are becoming more and more predominant with the rapid economic growth, urbanization and population expansion in most part of the region; and last but not least, (e) lack of an effective institutional framework for integrated and participatory water resources planning and management, a common difficulty in East Asian countries with fragmented sector-based management organizations and inadequate cross-sector coordination, collaboration and stakeholder involvement.

# CHAPTER 3

# Defining the Green Water Defense Approach

## Working Definition

The Green Water Defense (GWD) has been developed as an extension of the 'Green Growth' concept in the water sector. GWD is an adaptive management philosophy and approach which seeks to spatially integrate natural forces and human interventions, and to balance incentive-based and supply-driven measures, with minimum footprints and externalities in sustainably providing water services and managing related climate risks. It is enlightened by the green growth thinking and builds on a number of concepts and approaches, including: (a) Live with nature and build with nature; (b) Low impact development and green adaptation; (c) Integrated river basin & coastal zone management; (d) Productivity-based agricultural water management; and (e) Water-sensitive design and eco-dynamic design. The key GWD approaches to water resources management (see figure 3.1) are: (a) Managing water scarcity through 'Produce More with Less'; (b) Reducing flood risk under changing climate through 'Green Flood Defense'; (c) Achieving multiple co-benefits through 'Total Water Management'; and (d) Sustaining water management system through 'Water Sensitive Design'.

Conceptually, GWD can be illustrated by a simple spatial model (see figure 3.2) that consists of three spatial layers—the Base Layer (representing the ecosystem—air, water

Figure 3.1: Key GWD approaches to water resources management

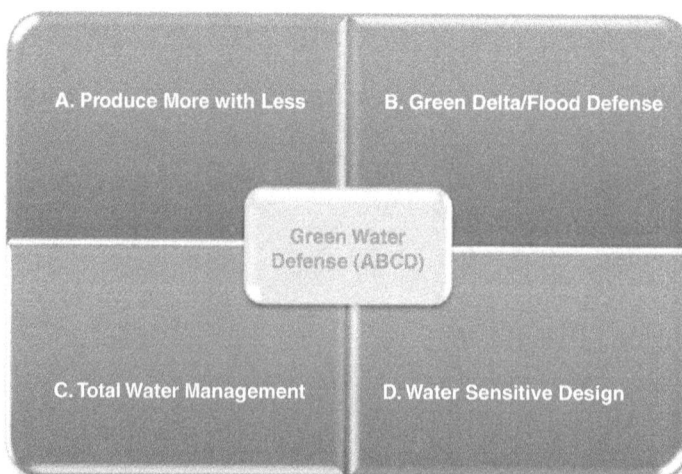

A. Produce More with Less

B. Green Delta/Flood Defense

Green Water Defense (ABCD)

C. Total Water Management

D. Water Sensitive Design

*Source:* Authors

**Figure 3.2: GWD overall conceptual framework**

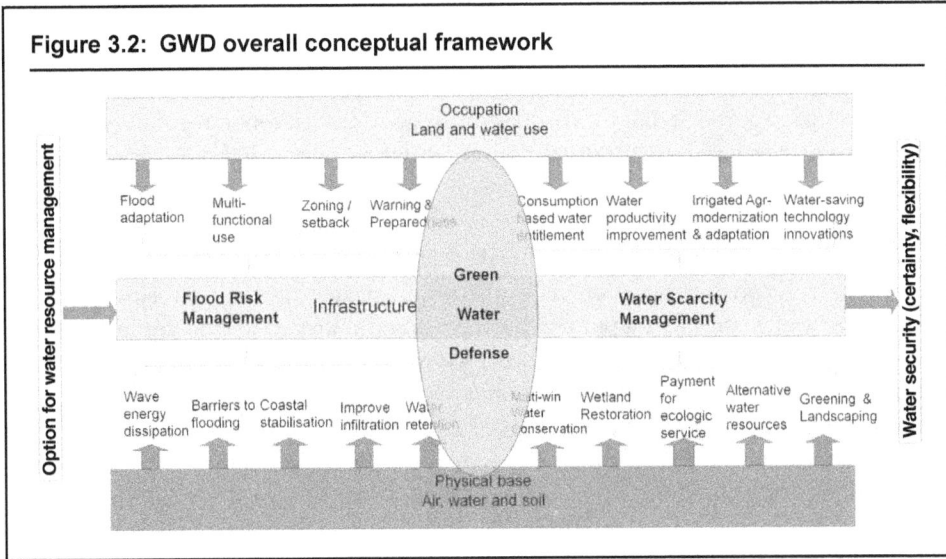

*Source:* Authors

and soil), the Network Layer (representing the infrastructure system) and the Occupation Layer (representing the human actions in land & water use), each with different and interrelated temporal dynamics and public-private involvement (VROM 2001). The model indicates a physical hierarchy in which the Base Layer influences the other layers through enabling and constraining factors, similar to the dynamic interactions and connections among economy, society and environment. For instance, the soil type in the Base Layer determines to a large extent the kind of agriculture that can be performed in the Occupation Layer. Unfavorable conditions (constraints) posed by the Base Layer can be mitigated through adaptations in the Network Layer and/or Occupation Layer. The GWD approach seeks to promote dynamic and healthy interactions among the three layers in an integrated manner, to achieve sustainability of the ecosystem, and of water and land use in providing the required services and managing related climate risks. Contrary to the conventional approach, GWD makes full use of the ecosystem services and balances structural and non-structural measures based on cost-effectiveness.

This report focuses on GWD approach to water scarcity management. In this regard, successful implementation of GWD is expected to have the following outcomes:

- The **certainty** of water available for use;
- The **flexibility** for water users to adjust to changing commodity demands and climate variability;
- The ability to **reallocate** scarce water supplies to benefit all users;
- The **security** of the amount available to users over time; and
- Environmental **sustainability** for water systems.

## Managing Water Scarcity through GWD

Sustainable management of water resources, whether it is scarce or not, requires using a range of both non-structural and structural measures, such as establishing a water entitlement system and distributing water through a piped rather than open channeled network where possible. Selection of the right measures requires an understanding of the status of the water resource to determine if it is under-developed, approaching fully allocated or over-allocated. The scarcer the water resource, the greater the need for a more strategic approach that incorporates a range of institutional, regulatory and infra-structural (natural and artificial) management measures to protect the resource. Basic starting knowledge should be defining water resource boundary and the annual water availability and water use, assessing if the resource is under-fully-or-over-allocated.

Potential climate variability and climate change impacts must be understood and fac-tored into decision-making in order to select optimal management measures. Measures must assist water users to adapt to both expected and unexpected changes in water avail-ability. As the risk of water scarcity increases, greater focus should be on implementing measures that provide a range of options to assist water users to find an appropriate response based on their own circumstances. Ensuring ecological services can continue to be provided to support the sustainability of water systems requires emphasis on the mainte-nance of important environmental assets and basic ecological health. Part of this process is to increase water users' understanding of both the reliability of water supply under differ-ent climate and demand scenarios as well as the potential impacts of reduced water avail-ability on the environment.

The water scarcity management conceptual framework (see figure 3.3), a subset of the GWD overall conceptual framework shown in figure 3.2 summarizes key GWD (non-structural and structural) measures and knowledge requirements for managing water resources. This framework places the measures in relation to the extent of scar-city of the water resource. Apparently, the scarcer the resource, the greater the number

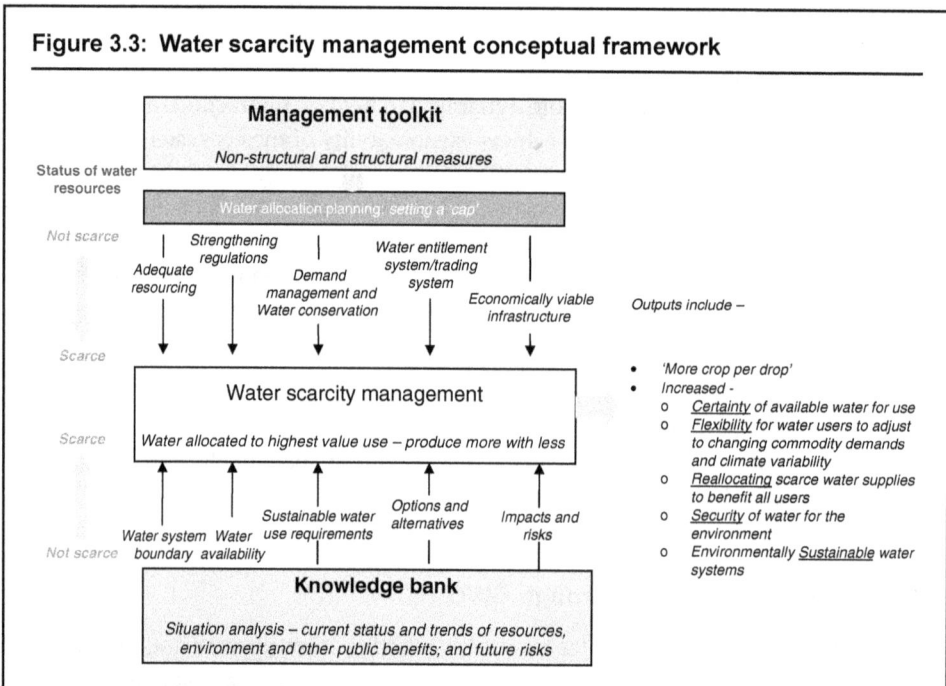

Figure 3.3: Water scarcity management conceptual framework

*Source:* Graeme Turner, 2012

of measures that must be implemented and the greater knowledge required to increase the certainty, flexibility and security of water for use. These measures are expected to lead to stronger green water defense, resulting in conservation of the resource as the value, both productive and monetary, and security of water increases for all users including the environment. The key elements of the conceptual framework are discussed below.

### Knowledge Bank (Base) for Understanding Current Status and Trends

Determining the water resource availability and whether it is under-fully-or-over-allocated requires considerable information. Good quality climate, biological and socioeconomic data is needed to assess supply limits, environmental flow needs and water use values. Long-term climate data and climate change projections are also important data requirements.

Those data are used to assess how much water is available for use, the types of water demands and whether water use is at a sustainable level or requires adjustment, as well as the scope for adjustment. The data is also used to determine the most efficient and cost effective mechanisms for improving the security of supply.

#### WATER SYSTEM BOUNDARY

Ideally, the water system boundary should be set at definable physical limits such as catchment, aquifer or river basin limits which recognize water flow paths and interconnection of definable water resources. If possible, political or administrative boundaries should be less important in determining the system boundaries.

#### WATER AVAILABILITY AND USE—WATER ACCOUNTING

The available water for use from a water system is generally determined by simulating the flows of the system under various demands using the longest period of inflow and climatic records available, or in some cases, longer periods of records based on statistically determined record extension. This simulation provides an indication of the minimum demands that can be met over various degrees of water scarcity. Climate variability also must be factored into the assessment, as it will have long-lasting effect on water availability. Climate variability can be viewed in two ways: (a) the natural temporal variations (e.g., annual and decadal) of these climate elements and (b) the permanent increase in the magnitude and frequency of changes to these elements as a result of industrial activities over the past 100 years or so (known as "climate change") (Bates et al. 2010). Understanding the current and potential extent of climate variability and its effect on water availability is necessary for assisting water managers and individual water users to prepare for potential changes to supply.

Supply-demand water balance assessments should include the following:

- Plausible climate (rainfall, temperature and evaporation) change predictions over a suitable planning period;
- Appropriate rainfall-runoff predictions to match the range of climate models under consideration;
- Water demand simulation models; and
- Determining levels of uncertainty for the water supply and demand scenarios under consideration.

#### SUSTAINABLE WATER USE REQUIREMENTS

Healthy aquatic ecosystems must be preserved to protect human health. The links between these two include provision of drinking water, food, waste disposal and cultural requirements (MEA 2005). As such, adequate provision of water for environmental use is necessary to ensure sustainable consumptive (agricultural, urban and industrial) water use.

Investigations will determine ecological values of a water system, their potential services and their water regime requirements (e.g., volume, timing and duration). Modeling analysis will determine the natural flow patterns of a water system, prior to any regulation. These flow patterns then can act as guide for setting an environmental flow provision to ensure sustainable consumptive use.

IMPACT AND RISK

This knowledge must be gained, including type and extent of potential impacts and risk, summarized and ordered to factor these events into allocation decision-making processes. Examples of risk to water availability include climate change and variability, increased extraction, interception activities such as dams in small catchment, land use change and forest generation after bushfires. Risk assessments can clearly identify the threatened asset (e.g., wetland, floodplain, local recreational water body), the probability of the threat, the potential extent (e.g., financial, aesthetic) of the threat and response options.

### Management Toolkit: Structural and Nonstructural Measures

WATER ALLOCATION PLANNING AND SETTING A CAP AND THE TRADE-OFF PROCESS

The prime function of water planning is to allocate a varying quantity of water available between various users (e.g., towns, irrigators, environment and recreation, etc.) over a period of time. Water plans are usually at the catchment scale, but can include multiple catchments (see box 3.1). They are established for regulated, unregulated, groundwater and surface water systems.

Two key elements of planning are setting a cap or upper use limit of the available water for use, and establishing a trade-off process for determining how the available water is to be shared and allocated between competing interests. These elements are important first steps for dealing with potential or existing water scarcity and provide a way for restricting use while maintaining a level of security of supply.

Setting the cap is usually guided by historic water use information, environmental values and community values. A number of mechanisms can be used to establish the trade-off process. However, flexibility of choice for individuals or groups should be part of this process.

---

**Box 3.1: Water planning in Australia**

In Australia there are currently three main types of water plans for controlling how, who, when and where water is used—those are:

- Only rules-based[1] (non-volumetric allocation) and do not incorporate entitlements (e.g. La Grange Groundwater Allocation Plan, Western Australia).
- Rules-based and include entitlements (volumetric allocation) (e.g. Lower River Murray Water Allocation Plan, South Australia).
- Only based on issuing of entitlements (e.g. Bulk Entitlement Conversion Orders for the Goulburn, Victoria).

*Adequate Resourcing.* Sustainable water resource management requires not only weighing a range of management options, but also ensuring at the start of planning stage that there are appropriate resources available to be able to effectively implement the agreed approach. Types of resources include finance, labor, expertise, time and ongoing political support. For example, establishing a multi-stakeholder participation governance structure, as supported by the GWD concept, requires factoring in a range of resources such as funding for access to experts and stakeholder support, etc. Successful implementation of the recommendations from a management group, such as establishing an on-going river health monitoring program, requires further resources.

*Strengthening Institutions and Regulations.* Strong and clearly defined institutional arrangements and regulations are essential so that organizations and individuals do not claim an unfettered right to water. Without these arrangements, water resources will likely be overexploited, eventually leading to severe shortages. Sustainable management of water resources requires strong government institutions, legislation and long-term planning capacity.

Water resource legislation can be strengthened by recognizing water sharing (e.g., water entitlements and a trading system), the role of water authorities, environmental requirements, climate change impacts, and monitoring of consumption. Successful implementation of any such legislation strengthening measures relies on public support.

Many government ministries, councils, departments, agencies and management boards may oversee a wide range of water related activities resulting in duplication, ambiguity over roles and general inefficiency. The roles and responsibilities of institutions must be clearly defined, integrated and aligned to outcomes. Water service provision should be separated from resource management, standard setting and regulatory enforcement to avoid conflicts of interest.

Initial focus should also be on raising awareness of the sustainable water sharing process and its benefits; understanding current and potential water availability, the types of water users and their current and potential use and establishing a clear process to issue water entitlements, including provisions for the environment.

*Water Entitlement System and Trading.* A water entitlement system is the core mechanism for managing water systems where demand is, or has the potential to be, greater than the supply. Water entitlements should be underpinned by legal authorization and specification of the amount of water to be stored, taken and used by an entity (e.g., irrigators, environmental water managers and water authorities). In a market based approach to reallocate water, the entitlement should be exclusive (i.e., separate from land ownership), able to be traded, enforceable and recorded in a publicly-accessible water register. Water resources should be allocated seasonally against the entitlement, based on a percentage of available inflows and existing storage levels.

Equitable sharing of available water requires good water resource accounting and management of water data, particularly where water is scarce and sharing arrangements apply between various users. Water use must be measured (preferably through a meter), regularly monitored and reported. Standardizing these processes improves coordination of data collection and management to facilitate sharing of information and an objective assessment of the sustainability of a water supply system.

Accurate metering and reporting also improve confidence of both water users and the broader community in the effectiveness of an entitlement system for managing scarce water resources by ensuring their prescribed allocation each season and demonstrating their right to an entitlement over time. As a result, the resource will be fully valued and used more productively, particularly when supply is low.

The type of measurement will depend on the available resources for a system (e.g., finance, technical expertise and labor), the level of demand and the extent, or potential extent, of the water system degradation. In the rural context, particularly for large irrigation systems, it is necessary to measure the volume of inflows, water storage levels, entitlement holders' use (e.g., irrigators, town supply and environment) and distribution network losses.

*Publicly Accessible Water Registers.* Publicly accessible water registers record entitlement ownership details, total entitlement volume, seasonal allocation allowed against the entitlement, on-going and seasonal allocation used, volumes traded and price paid. Water is progressively deducted from the allocation to the entitlement holder, and is not supplied if the allocation is exhausted; severe penalties apply for unauthorized water use.

Using water registers increases transparency and accountability of water use, building confidence in water markets and in the equitable management of scarce water resources. Water registers can also reduce market transaction costs, streamline entitlement registration and trading and provide reliable information for water planning decisions.

*Economically Viable Infrastructure for Efficiency Improvement in Irrigation.* Water losses in water supply and distribution systems can be significant for agricultural and urban uses. In irrigation water supply systems, the transmission losses between the storage and the plant root zone, depending on the size and condition of the infrastructure, can be higher than 60 percent. Investments in improving and modernizing water supply infrastructure to reduce losses and improve the efficiency of supply are among the crucial measures to improve water availability and particularly important in circumstances where periods of water scarcity are expected to increase.

Irrigation system modernization falls into three levels as follows:

- Improving the efficiency and operation of the headworks system (storages to irrigation distribution off takes);
- Upgrading and modernizing irrigation distribution systems (canal/channel network from off take points to farm); and
- Upgrading on-farm works to improve efficiency of supply and water savings (delivery of water from farm off-take to plants/crops).

The type of investment in efficiency improvements depends on analyzing the type of losses and their quantification to ensure the cost effectiveness of investment. In headworks systems most losses can be attributed to evaporation, although losses can be high where water is transferred via river systems to irrigation off-takes downstream. Upgrading operating practices associated with the transfer of water can reduce losses and, in some cases, it is possible to achieve substantial evaporation savings from off-river storages by partitioning (reducing surface area) or even decommissioning the storage where practical.

Losses in irrigation distribution systems are caused by evaporation, seepage, leakage, channel spills through outfall structures, theft and over-supply through poor measurement. Poor measurement does not necessarily result in a loss of water to productive use; however, it does lead to inequities in the sharing of water.

Generally, pipelining is the most efficient means of reducing losses, although costs can be prohibitive and thus not practical for larger open channel systems. For larger irrigation systems, the most promising options to improve the efficiency of supply are upgrading channels and modernizing channel control structures to improve measurement and automate the delivery of water to farms. Experience has shown that these works must be accompanied by measures to ensure that the targeted improvements are achieved and sustained in the longer term, including on-going measurement of supply efficiencies and reforms to ensure that costs of maintaining the upgraded system are recovered and that the entitlement system incorporates incentives, e.g., requiring the distribution system manager to be held accountable for maintaining future efficiency.

Improvements in the supply efficiency often lead to a reduction in return flows back to river systems or in accessions to groundwater aquifers. This outcome must be considered when planning efficiency improvements from both environmental and water supply perspectives, particularly where return flows or groundwater accessions augment other sources of supply or provide an environmental benefit.

In many cases, the environmental consequences of continuing return flows and accessions can be significant. Irrigation runoff from farms can wash the nutrients back into river systems, causing algal blooms and deterioration of water quality. Similarly, significant salinity and land degradation are consequences of excessive groundwater accessions from poor irrigation practices. The nature of improvement depends on the size of farm, existing irrigation practices and types of crops being irrigated.

DEMAND MANAGEMENT AND WATER CONSERVATION

Demand management refers to policy and management interventions that stress making better use of existing supplies and curtailing water consumption by changing users' behaviors in water use. Such measures include water pricing, subsidy programs, participatory management, awareness raising and education programs, etc. Water conservation includes water saving, loss reduction, recycling and reuse, and protection of water quality and water-dependent ecosystems.

*Evapo-Transpiration (ET) Management for 'Real' Water Savings.* ET management targets reducing water consumption (e.g., in irrigated agriculture), by minimizing water losses in the form of non-beneficial ET. Most water "saved" by conventional approach would have returned to the aquifers below and contributed to keep dynamic balance of groundwater storage. However, 'saved' water used for irrigation expansion, actually increases the water consumption. Therefore, in agricultural systems, water in a hydrologic system is truly lost through Evapo-Transpiration (ET): water evaporated from water and land surfaces and transpired from plant leaves into the atmosphere. For example, growing more crops over a wider irrigated area or increasing cropping intensity in the same irrigation area would raise the level of ET. In an agricultural system, improved ET management reduces water assumption through a combination of engineering, agricultural and management measures (see Chapter 4 for details). ET management and water productivity improvement are the most critical GWD measures in agricultural water management and conservation.

## A Menu of GWD Measures for Adaptive Water Management

The GWD framework incorporates a broad range of green growth oriented management approaches and measures for water management, as shown in the concept framework, although not all measures are suited for all scale levels. To illustrate the utility of the GWD approach, a menu of indicative GWD measures for water scarcity management is as follows (tables 3.1–3.3 below), with grouping by spatial scales and management mechanisms as well as the three spatial layers. This menu provides a broad reference for selecting measures appropriate for particular circumstances.

**Table 3.1:  A menu of GWD measures at the river basin level**

| Management unit | Mechanism | Spatial layer | GWD measures |
|---|---|---|---|
| River basin | Catchment management | Land and water use | • Multi-stakeholder river basin organization<br>• Water resources (availability and scarcity) assessment, climate outlook and flow forecasting<br>• Integrated land-water-environment management planning<br>• Basin strategic plan and water supply master plan<br>• Groundwater management zoning & use plan<br>• Water quality management plan |
| | | Infrastructure | • Essential water regulation/storage and management infrastructure<br>• Watershed management (soil & water conservation) works<br>• Waterway management works<br>• Salinity control works<br>• A rational hydro-met monitoring network |
| | | Physical base | • Afforestation/reforestation<br>• Wetlands/swamps ecological requirements<br>• Aquifer monitoring and development management |
| | Water allocation | Land and water use | • Water accounting (water availability, entitlement, supply/use register)<br>• Water sharing and use plan (especially for trans-boundary rivers)<br>• Regulations on allocation, trade/transfer and reallocation<br>• Water withdrawal permit/licensing system<br>• Intra-basin transfer and trade |
| | | Infrastructure | • Water withdrawal, conveyance and distribution infrastructure<br>• Water control and measurement facilities |
| | | Physical base | • Allocation for environment<br>• Eco-system preservation |
| | Water conservation | Land and water Use | • Integrated water-environment management plan for each jurisdiction in the basin<br>• Incentive policies for water conservation<br>• Consumption (ET) based water allocation system<br>• Demand management (e.g. water resources tax and water use charges)<br>• Water use cap and rationing<br>• Restrictions on unregulated diversions<br>• well-drilling and groundwater withdrawal permit<br>• Conservation agriculture and eco-farming |
| | | Infrastructure | • Water conservation infrastructure for different uses<br>• Water consumption monitoring facilities<br>• Production-focused water supply system modernization<br>• Irrigation technological improvement<br>• Water quality monitoring network |
| | | Physical base | • Targeted water conservation programs for different use sectors<br>• Soil erosion control interventions<br>• Water pollution (point and non-point sources) control<br>• Payment for ecological services |
| | Supply augmentation | Land and water use | • Source diversification—alternative water sources for portable & non-portable uses<br>• Rain/storm water harvesting<br>• Surface—ground water conjunctive use and brackish water utilization |
| | | Infrastructure | • Multi-functional storage reservoir<br>• Retention and infiltration basins<br>• Intra-basin transfers (between riparian)<br>• Infrastructure/technology investments for real-water saving and water reallocation |
| | | Physical base | • River/water body water quality monitoring and control<br>• (Treated) wastewater utilization and trade (with freshwater)<br>• Virtual basin management and virtual water trade<br>• Drought response plan and climate-indexed insurance |

*Source:* Authors

**Table 3.2: A menu of GWD measures at the agricultural water system level**

| Management unit | Mechanism | Spatial layer | GWD measures |
|---|---|---|---|
| Agricultural water system | System management | Land and water use | • Consumption-based agric. water management<br>• Participatory irrigation management<br>• Restrictions on unregulated water withdrawal<br>• Agricultural policy (e.g. land use, water charge)<br>• Crop diversification |
| | | Infrastructure | • Irrigation system modernization<br>• Irrigation supply efficiency improvement works<br>• Asset management: risk-based operations and maintenance of Irrigation and drainage structures |
| | | Physical base | • Climate change adaptation in irrigated agriculture<br>• Groundwater recharge and use management<br>• Soil (fertility) conservation and improvement |
| | Water allocation | Land and water use | • Water allocation plan and entitlement system<br>• Seasonal allocations to entitlement holders<br>• ET target (quota) allocation<br>• Water use licensing and permit<br>• Water reallocation and entitlement trading<br>• Regulations on land reclamation and expansion |
| | | Infrastructure | • Water regulation, distribution and control works and technologies<br>• Water measuring/monitoring devices (e.g., IC) |
| | | Physical base | • Water allocation for environmental use and irrigation return flow measurement<br>• Water consumption and groundwater monitoring<br>• Trading/transfer of water saved |
| | Water conservation | Land and water use | • Awareness raising and 'water-conservation society' campaign<br>• Incentive policy for water efficient production<br>• Targeted water conservation program<br>• System of rice intensification (SRI) & eco-farming<br>• Deficit irrigation<br>• Drought-resistant crop varieties<br>• Land leveling/grading<br>• Soil moisture preservation<br>• Water demand management<br>• Volumetric water charges |
| | | Infrastructure | • Irrigation canal upgrading and pipelining<br>• On-farm water-saving works and technologies<br>• Groundwater recharge and infiltration |
| | | Physical base | • Triple-win water saving techniques<br>• Groundwater level control<br>• NPS nutrient/pollutant control (e.g. Eco-drains)<br>• Climate-smart & Conservation agriculture<br>• Balanced fertilizer application |
| | Supply augmentation | Land and water use | • Virtual water trade through food trade<br>• Rainwater harvesting and runoff interception<br>• Irrigation return flow utilization<br>• Alternative water sources (reclaimed wastewater) |
| | | Infrastructure | • Rainwater harvesting and conjunctive use facilities<br>• Watershed management<br>• On-farm storage |
| | | Physical base | • Local brackish water utilization<br>• Drought emergency supply & management plan |

*Source:* Authors

**Table 3.3: A menu of GWD measures at the urban (city) system level**

| Management unit | Mechanism | Spatial layer | GWD measures |
|---|---|---|---|
| City | Catchment management | Land and water use | • Total water management strategy<br>• Participatory spatial planning and risk-informed land and water use plan<br>• Multi-stakeholder water governance<br>• Integrated urban water (cycle) management<br>• Urban watershed management (e.g. green space)<br>• Water/river/eco-city initiatives<br>• Policies for promoting low water-consumption and low pollution industries |
| | | Infrastructure | • Water sensitive water management system<br>• Climate-resilient infrastructure<br>• Separate stormwater and sewage systems<br>• Green buildings and permeable pavements |
| | | Physical base | • Multiple (consumptive and non-consumptive) use of water<br>• Preservation of natural hydrological regimes<br>• Greening parks and (water) gardens<br>• Ecological restoration of streams<br>• In-stream water treatment<br>• Vertical landscaping |
| | Water allocation | Land and water use | • Water entitlement and permit/licensing system<br>• Water right trading and water bank/market<br>• Runoff interception and artificial recharge |
| | | Infrastructure | • Water regulation and control structures<br>• Water metering and measurement facilities<br>• Runoff interception and groundwater recharge facilities |
| | | Physical base | • Water allocation for environment<br>• Soil/land erosion control<br>• Environmental flow and water quality monitoring |
| | Water conservation | Land and water use | • Water demand management (e.g. through differentiated water tariffs)<br>• Supply/distribution loss (leakage) reduction<br>• Non-revenue water (NRW) reduction<br>• Sewage discharge permit and trading<br>• Landscape management to reduce outdoor water consumption |
| | | Infrastructure | • Wastewater collection and treatment<br>• Water efficient appliances and water-saving facilities<br>• Clean production technology<br>• Constructed multipurpose wetlands |
| | | Physical base | • Minimizing wastewater generation<br>• Pollution abatement and treatment (through wetlands)<br>• Water reclamation<br>• Urban waterway health improvement/restoration |
| | Supply augmentation | Land and water use | • Alternative water sources for portable and non-portable uses<br>• Water recycle, reuse and reclamation<br>• Utilization of flood/storm water |
| | | Infrastructure | • Water supply infrastructure (new and upgrading)<br>• Multi-functional infrastructure<br>• Retention ponds and underground reservoirs<br>• Canal/stream storage<br>• Optimal operation of water source works |
| | | Physical base | • Preservation of water sources<br>• Groundwater monitoring and management<br>• Water trade with rural water users<br>• Rainwater, grey water and black water reuse |

*Source:* Authors

# CHAPTER 4

# Selected Country Case Studies

## Australia: The Cases of Victoria and Sydney

*Victoria: Northern Victoria, Goulburn-Murray River Basin, Irrigation System Levels*

Australia is renowned for its highly variable climate, demonstrated by the rainfall records that date back more than 100 years. Similar to East Asia, Australia's land mass covers a range of climates including the tropical north, temperate south and east regions and the desert and semi-arid regions in the center. Except for the far north and south regions (i.e., west coast of Tasmania), where annual rainfall can exceed 2,000 mm, Australia's rainfall is relatively low and variable, with an annual average rainfall of less than 600 mm (CSIRO 2008). The increasing demand for water, decreasing water availability and societal need for greater security and certainty to water have been overarching drivers that have led to major water reforms in Australia since 1994. Under Australia's Federal System, the seven states and two territory governments have the constitutional responsibility for water resource management. The Federal government, however, has progressively increased its focus on water reform since the mid-1990, primarily as a result of the extended drought in south-eastern Australia, which includes the Murray Darling Basin. Influence from the Council of Australian Governments led to the separation of land and water and the establishment of water as a tradable right in 1994. The signing of the National Water Initiative agreement (2004), through which all jurisdictions acknowledged the importance of water allocation plans, and the need for efficient water markets and pricing mechanisms. The National Water Act (2007) was the first time that water for environmental and basic human needs in the Murray-Darling Basin was given a higher priority than any other users.

These federal reforms have trickled down to the relevant state and territory water acts and strategic policies. As a result, all states and territories have established water entitlement, allocation and trading systems, and are implementing approximately 150 water sharing plans (NWC, 2011b). The water entitlement system and trading are the core mechanisms for managing water systems. Trading water entitlements and water allocations between different entities allows water to be used at its highest value, i.e., most productively. Trading gives water users the opportunity to plan ahead, respond and adapt to existing and potential changes in water availability, to best meet their own circumstances and avoids the problems governments' picking 'winners and losers' (NWC, 2011). These management measures enable reallocating scarce water resources to its highest value use and ensuring high productivity of water.

The recent drought in south-eastern Australia has led to significant investment to ensure long term sustainability of water resources and required major adjustments. The most significant measure was the Federal Government's $A12 billon 'Water for the Future' initiative for improving sustainable water use in the Murray-Darling Basin. Key features of this initiative include purchasing water for the environment, improving irrigation efficiency and developing alternative water sources (DSEWPC 2011), all discussed in more detail below.

CHALLENGES AND DRIVERS

The Murray-Darling Basin (MDB) is located on the eastern part of Australia and crosses four states and one territory. It provides over one-third of Australia's food supply and generates 39 percent of national income derived from agricultural production. The MDB system in northern Victoria consists of eight catchments. On average, 91% of total water use is from surface water, 5% from groundwater and 4% from alternative sources. Total surface water resources for the region is approximately 10,230 GL/year of which approximately 4,090 GL/year is used for consumptive use (i.e., 96% for irrigation, 4% for urban areas).

Between 1997 and 2009, Victoria experienced unprecedented dry conditions—a period now known as the Millennium Drought. These 13 consecutive years of drought, including the lowest recorded annual inflows to storages (2006–07), resulted in conditions well outside the boundaries in which the water supply systems and water sharing rules across Victoria were designed to operate. By summer 2006–07, many areas faced severe water shortages. On average, the annual rainfall was 13 percent below the long-term average, and the major water storages held only 26 percent of long-term average volume by 2007.

While Victoria is experiencing a high level of seasonal and inter-annual rainfall variability, potential climate change impacts are likely to exacerbate these patterns, leading to warmer and drier weather and more frequent and prolonged droughts. In preparing the Northern Sustainable Water Strategy, five climate scenarios were modeled to better understand potential reductions in water availability: base case (long-term average, based on historical record); low, medium and high climate change predictions, and continuation of recent low inflows. All scenarios showed a potential significant reduction in total inflows across the region ranging from -5% (Kiewa River—low climate change) to 72% (Campaspe River—continuation of low inflows experienced in the recent drought) (DSE 2009). Evaporations also predicted to increase with most impact occurring in this region of Australia where rainfalls are already low and variable and extraction is high. This level of reduced water availability significantly impact water dependant ecosystems, irrigators, industry, towns and community activities.

Aside from climate change impacts, interception water use activities present a risk, if not managed appropriately, to the security of the water entitlement system by reducing the amount of water available to entitlement holders and the environment. Interception activities are generally those that use significant amounts of unaccounted water for consumptive purposes, capturing rainfall before it reaches the river or groundwater systems, including plantation forestry, floodplain harvesting, farm dams and stock and domestic use.

MANAGEMENT MEASURES: NONSTRUCTURAL

*Water Entitlement and Planning Frameworks.* Victoria's water entitlement and planning frameworks form the basis for water resources management in Victoria. These frameworks influence how a region deals with water scarcity and a region experiences water shortage. For example, Victoria's water entitlement framework has enabled secure water rights for different water uses. A legislated and integrated water planning framework supports and guides the management of water allocated under the entitlement framework (see box 4.1).

The water entitlement framework is a three-tiered system that provides the legal basis for water-sharing across the state (see figure 4.1). One of the principles underlying

## Box 4.1:  Victoria's water planning framework

Victoria's various water plans outline a 'vision' for future water use at different organizational levels (state-wide, regional, river basin, town) and across different timescales. For all water plans, the risks to the future water supply are considered at the development stage. This includes uncertainty created by climate change. Social drivers (e.g. demographic changes, population projections), economic drivers (e.g. future water demands) and environmental requirements are also identified and incorporated in the preparation of the plans. Community consultation is a legal requirement and an important part of the planning process for harnessing local wisdom to help foster 'ownership' of the plan's objectives. All water plans are subject to a formal review process to ensure that they remain relevant; consider best available information; and incorporate lessons learned in the intervening period. If a plan includes recommended actions, the review process provides an opportunity to examine progress against these actions.

**Box Figure 4.1.1:  Water plan review process**

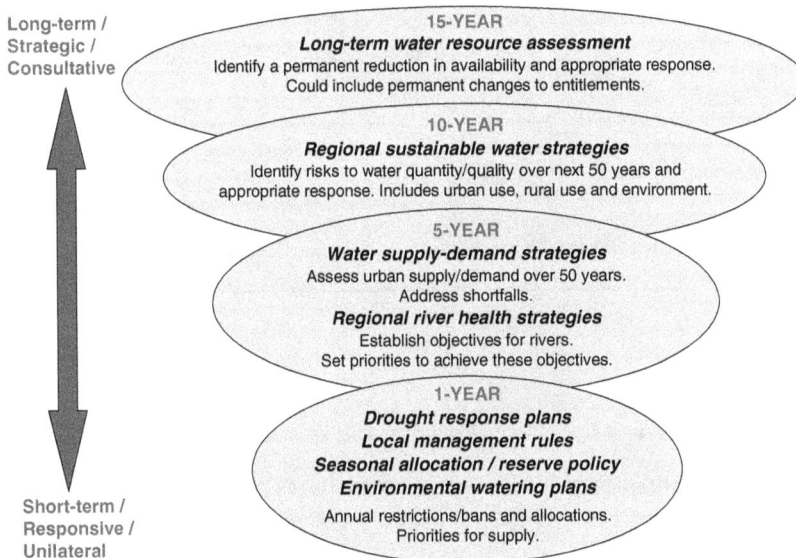

Long-term /
Strategic /
Consultative

**15-YEAR**
*Long-term water resource assessment*
Identify a permanent reduction in availability and appropriate response.
Could include permanent changes to entitlements.

**10-YEAR**
*Regional sustainable water strategies*
Identify risks to water quantity/quality over next 50 years and appropriate response. Includes urban use, rural use and environment.

**5-YEAR**
*Water supply-demand strategies*
Assess urban supply/demand over 50 years.
Address shortfalls.
*Regional river health strategies*
Establish objectives for rivers.
Set priorities to achieve these objectives.

**1-YEAR**
*Drought response plans*
*Local management rules*
*Seasonal allocation / reserve policy*
*Environmental watering plans*
Annual restrictions/bans and allocations.
Priorities for supply.

Short-term /
Responsive /
Unilateral

*Source:* Department of Sustainability and Environment, 2009

Victoria's water entitlement framework is that, where possible, water should be reallocated via market mechanisms rather than government intervention. Many of the water entitlements, such as high reliability and low reliability water shares, are tradable to other parties. This tradability ensures that water can move to its highest value use for higher productivity via voluntary market mechanisms, which provide monetary compensation to the willing water sellers.

In the regulated systems in Victoria, e.g., the northern region, water resources are allocated by bulk entitlements issued to rural and urban water corporations, and the Victorian environmental water holder, an independent government statutory body. Bulk entitlements are issued under the Victorian *Water Act 1989*, the basis for Victoria's water allocation and entitlement framework. Within the bulk entitlements held by rural water authorities, irrigators are issued individual (third-tier) entitlements as a share of the available resource. Bulk entitlements provide a practical and cost-effective way of sharing and managing limited resources.

**Figure 4.1: Victoria's water entitlement framework: hierarchy of water rights**

Reference Guide 1: Water Entitlements

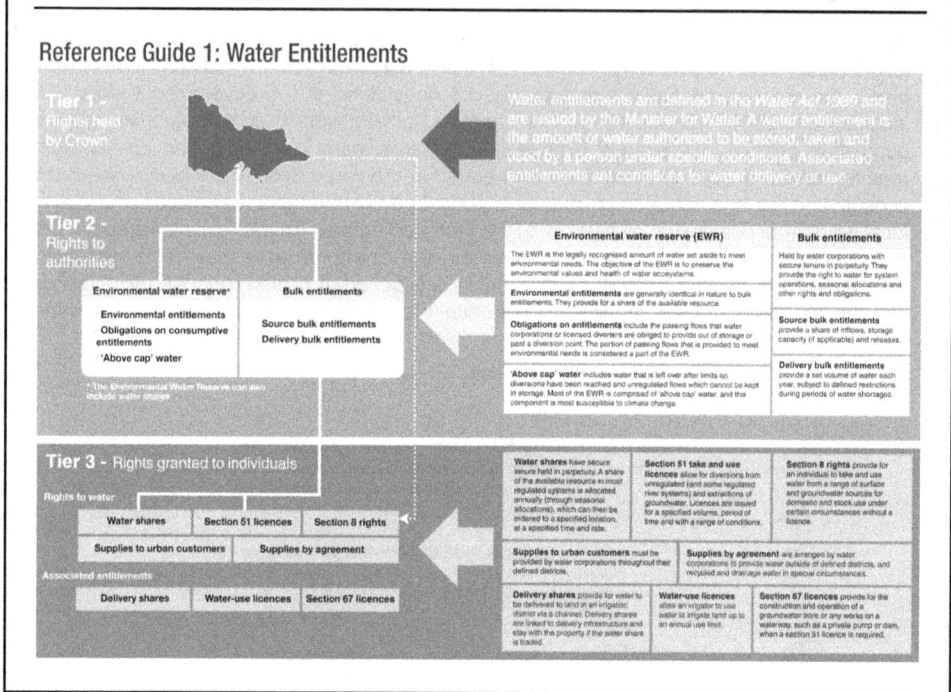

*Source:* Department of Sustainability and Environment, 2009

The key elements of the water allocation and entitlement framework are:

- Secure entitlements—with legal tenure that is certain and protected, including bulk entitlements, environmental entitlements, water shares, licenses, rights or contractual agreements to supply;
- Limits on water entitlements—that is, specified volumes, extraction rates and locations, diversion rules and sharing arrangements;
- Water allocation rules—how water is allocated annually against entitlements (see box 4.2);
- Clear consultative processes before entitlements are changed; and
- Ability to trade—using markets to facilitate efficient allocation of resources, giving water users the flexibility to buy and sell water.

A key principle of the water entitlement framework is that individual entitlement holders are responsible for managing the risks of water scarcity within their own contexts and systems.

Bulk entitlements define the specific nature and annual volume for a water entitlement (e.g., systems operating water to meet losses, irrigation, pipeline use, recreation and environment) in a water system or systems. In some cases, they also direct water authorities to prepare storage management operating rules to ensure a certain level of reliability of entitlement water delivery. The final step is issuing individual water shares (primarily to irrigators) as a share of the resource within a bulk entitlement.

**Box 4.2:  Water sharing rules**

Water sharing rules are prepared by and agreed to by all interested parties on how available water is issued between the various entitlement holders within a water system, including rules for allocation during water shortages. Setting these rules up-front assists water users to understand how water is distributed as a result of reduced water availability, including extreme reductions, and to be better able to manage their risks such as establishing their own contingency measures. These rules are specified bulk and environment entitlements. The storage manager allocates the available water in the system using the water sharing rules.

**Box Table 4.2.1:  Sample of a water sharing plan**

| Water entitlement product | Entitlement volume/per year (ML) | Available water (ML) | | | | |
|---|---|---|---|---|---|---|
| | | A | B | C | D | E |
| | | 125,550 | 97,550 | 75,971 | 53,459 | 45,253 |
| **Grampians Wimmera Mallee Water Corporation** | | | | | | |
| System operating water | | | | | | |
| - Irrigation losses | 9,000 | 100% | 0% | 0% | 0% | 0% |
| - Pipeline and balancing storage losses | 2,960 | 100% | 100% | 100% | 100% | 100% |
| Irrigation product | 19,000 | 100% | 0% | 0% | 0% | 0% |
| Glenelg compensation flow | 3,300 | 100% | 100% | 25% | 1.5% | 1.5% |
| Recreation | 2,590 | 100% | 100% | 25% | 0% | 0% |
| Wimmera-Mallee Pipeline product | 44,720 | 100% | 100% | 81.3% | 57.5% | 48.2% |
| **Coliban Water Corporation** | | | | | | |
| Wimmera-Mallee Pipeline product | 300 | 100% | 100% | 81.3% | 57.5% | 48.2% |
| **Victorian Environmental Water Holder** | | | | | | |
| Wetlands | 1,000 | 100% | 100% | 25% | 0% | 0% |
| Wimmera-Mallee Pipeline product | 40,560 | 100% | 100% | 81.3% | 57.5% | 48.2% |

*Source:* Sample Table of Water Sharing Rules taken from the Wimmera-Mallee system explanatory note for bulk and environmental entitlements

Specific entitlements can also be granted, for only environmental use. Most of these environmental entitlements are issued to and are the responsibility of the federal or state government agencies. These entitlements provide environmental water to improve biodiversity, ecological functioning and quality of water, and in particular, maintain important ecological refuges and species during drought.

In regulated water supply systems, bulk entitlements and environmental entitlements provide holders a right to shares of a percentage of inflows and storage capacity where water is harvested. Entitlement holders may have storage shares different from inflows shares, and inflow shares that vary between months and seasons. The separation of inflow and storage shares provides holders with more flexibility for managing their entitlement. For example, as a contingency measure against a potential extended dry season, an entitlement holder may purchase more inflow than storage shares to minimize their risk of reduced seasonal water allocations.

Bulk entitlements and environmental entitlements require storage management rules for water management within and transfer between storages in a water supply system. These rules prescribe the order of release for different categories of water use within a storage system under different water availability scenarios. This process provides another layer of security to entitlement holders, as it gives them a clearer idea of available water allocation within the supply system, particularly when there are low inflows (see box 4.2).

Construction of large storages, unchecked extraction of water for consumption and limited formal provision for environmental requirements have affected the condition of the rivers, wetlands, floodplains and aquifers in the inland river systems of southeast Australia. The Sustainable rivers audit[1] undertaken in the Murray-Darling Basin found that the current condition of Victoria's northern rivers was poor. Ecological health had declined and towns and industries that depended on reliable, high-quality water were impacted. Victoria and other Murray-Darling Basin States responded by introducing a cap on annual water use and are investing in a range of projects to reallocate water from consumptive use to the environment. In addition, the Federal Government has intervened requiring a plan to sustainably manage the Basin.

Unlike surface water resources, the groundwater resources in northern Victoria are not over-allocated. However, as a precautionary measure, permissible consumptive volumes have been set on the total annual amount of water that can be extracted within the aquifer system.

Regulated systems (via dams, weirs and other flow-regulating structures) were designed to transform the natural variability of streamflows into a reliable supply of water for towns and irrigation. However, by 2007, following the lowest recorded inflows, many of the regulated systems no longer operated as designed or as the entitlement rules described. Even with contingency measures in place, there was not enough water to operate all or part of many regulated systems. Between 2007 and 2010, all northern regulated systems opened the season with zero allocations. The extreme water shortages required Victoria's water managers to demonstrate their resourcefulness in making the small amount of water available go further and ensuring it went to the most needy users.

In the northern irrigation systems in 2006–07, the Victorian government introduced the 'carryover' mechanism to provide irrigators with extra flexibility in managing their water entitlements by allowing unused water allocations to be kept in storages for use in the following season.

*Allocation/Entitlement Trading and Supporting Tools.* During the drought, new storage reserve rules reduced the risk of starting a new season with zero allocation. Even under severe drought, once enough water was available to make a small seasonal allocation, the well established water markets and supportive tools such as the water register (see box 4.3), enabled individual users to weigh up options based on their own circumstances and adjust their allocations via trading. This ensured that water rose to its highest value uses.

*Management Innovations to Maximize Ecological Benefits.* With less water available for the environment during the dry years, innovative approaches use the available water for maximum ecological benefits. These included building structural works to deliver environmental water more efficiently, making use of consumptive water en route to other destinations and changing the seasonal priority of environmental water needs and the delivery pattern of passing flows to achieve maximum environmental benefit.

Many modifications made to long-standing practices during the Millennium Drought (1997 to 2009) provided extra flexibility for water managers. New practices in normal system operations where possible help adapt to a possibly drier future.

## Box 4.3:  Victorian (Australia) Water Register

The Victoria's Water Register was set-up mid-2007 as a register of all water-related entitlements in Victoria. Its purpose is to build public and investor confidence in the water entitlement market by providing publicly accessible records of the amount of water being delivered, traded and extracted for consumptive, environmental and other public benefit uses. It is a particularly useful resource when water is scarce, assisting water users to understand what water is available for purchase, its location, reliability and cost; and the steps for making a trade.

Data from the register is also used for preparing annual summary reports, e.g., the Victoria Water Accounts report that provides an overview of annual water availability and use across Victoria. The report illustrates to water users the impacts of changing climates on water availability. Another report, the annual National Water Commission Australian Water Market report, draws on data from the registers in all states and territories of Australia, including the Victoria's Water Register. In summarizing all the trades, the report gives clear evidence that water trade has provided water users greater flexibility to respond to economic and climatic pressures across Australia.

The Victorian Water Register is currently being used as a blueprint for establishing an Australia-wide water register to facilitate interstate trading.

The register can be found at: http://waterregister.vic.gov.au/

### Box Figure 4.3.1:  Screenshot of the Victorian Water Register.

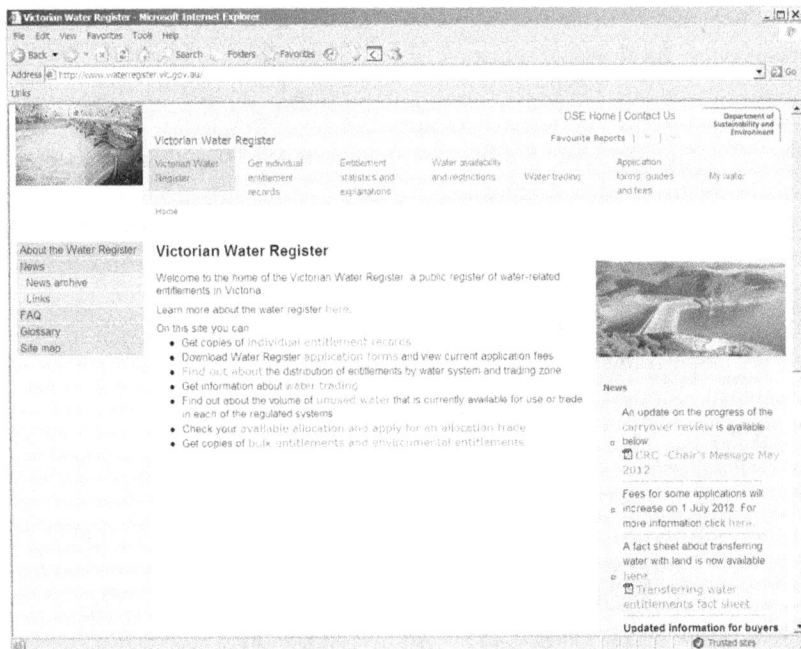

*Source:* www.waterregister.vic.gov.au/

*Demand Management and Alternative Water Sources.* The challenges to urban water corporations varied, depending on the nature of their supply systems. Only a handful of Victorian urban systems did not suffer the impact of the prolonged dry spell between 1997 and 2009. Many urban water corporations' first response was to reduce demand by imposing restrictions on residential customers and by working with large industrial customers to reduce demand. By July 2007, some 457 Victorian towns were subject to restrictions. In some cases, water was carted to towns on Stage 4 restrictions (the highest level of restriction) to meet essential needs if no other feasible supply options were available.

Urban water corporations realized that the duration and magnitude of the drought were worse than anything anticipated by their water supply-demand strategies or drought response plans. As the dry conditions intensified, the water corporations found that the water available to take under their bulk entitlements was insufficient to ensure supply to meet critical human needs of their urban communities. Furthermore, contingencies were not designed to cope with dry conditions of such nature and scale.

As a result, increased interest in alternative water sources such as recycled water, desalination, storm water and managed aquifer recharge has prompted consideration of allocating and accounting for these sources within the water entitlement framework.

*Progressive Restrictions on Unregulated Diversions.* Due to the lack of flow regulation on unregulated systems, water users had very little control over the amount of water available. Therefore, fewer options were available on unregulated systems for entitlement holders to manage their supplies during the Millennium Drought. Individuals who took water from unregulated streams (under licenses) for irrigation, commercial, domestic and stock uses were responsible for their own supply infrastructure. They did not have the benefit of large storages and interconnections with other systems to help secure their water supplies. As flows diminished, licensing authorities employed, wherever possible, progressive stages of restrictions on diversions for irrigation and commercial uses. Bans on taking water for irrigation ensured enough flow to supply critical needs for domestic, stock and the environment. From 2006–07 to 2009–10, licensed diverters around Victoria experienced restrictions and bans intermittently each year, and some streams maintained the bans throughout the year, and for consecutive years.

*Drought Emergency Supply and Management Measures.* Domestic and stock users across Victoria experienced significant water shortages and many users had to cart water to maintain supplies. Carting water is an expensive and time-consuming task and, as a result, extensive de-stocking of land occurred where it was not financially viable to cart water for significant periods.

The drought encouraged a significant increase in groundwater extractions across the state as people looked for other sources of supply. Demand for construction of new groundwater bores increased sharply. A significant number of the 16,000 new bore construction applications received between 2006 and 2009 were for domestic and stock use in rural areas. Also, many private bores were constructed in greater Melbourne to enable residents to water their gardens while normal supply was restricted.

The Victoria government enlarged the network of emergency water supply from 170 to 270 points across the state. Landholders faced with almost empty reservoirs, not able to pump from streams or access groundwater, carted water from these emergency supply points.

Passing flows make up most environmental water in the unregulated systems, which generally stem from obligations on other users. In some unregulated systems, the passing flow rules were temporarily qualified to alleviate stress on towns and private diverters by allowing them to divert some water when the streams were running lower than the historical passing flow requirements.

Victoria's water management arrangements pledged responsibility on water entitlement holders to manage through droughts. However, in exceptional circumstances when water-sharing arrangements are no longer adequate to meet entitlement holders' basic needs, the Minister can intervene to declare a water shortage and qualify rights temporarily.

Before 2006, only a handful of qualifications had been approved under the Act, and no clear process had been established for applying. In response to demands for qualifications during the Millennium Drought, the Victorian Department of Sustainability and Environment prepared guidelines for water corporations and agencies to request a qualification of rights in 2008. The guidelines define when a qualification is appropriate, specify the priority of supply to different user groups under the qualification and assign responsibility for reporting on the effectiveness of the qualification and paying the costs of monitoring and managing the impact of the qualification on third parties. In many cases, rights were qualified during the drought as a stop-gap measure to ensure water corporations could continue to supply their customers' critical needs until longer-term measures to secure supplies were in place.

In rural areas, such as the Broken River system, qualification of rights enabled domestic and stock customers to access water for their livestock. Rights were qualified to provide waterway managers with more flexibility to help reduce the impact of the drought on river health. Preparing all proposals to qualify rights involved consultation with major stakeholders to ensure the qualification minimizes impacts on other water users and the environment. Impacts on other water users and the environment were identified and assessed, and all parties made aware of their financial, monitoring and reporting responsibilities. Scientific advice on the environmental risks involved guided decisions to qualify rights.

The experience gained in preparing qualifications of rights across the state in a variety of situations allowed improvements to the qualification process. Successive qualifications take advantage of better knowledge of operating systems and managing environmental impacts under extreme dry conditions, reducing the need for qualification of rights in future dry periods.

MANAGEMENT MEASURES: STRUCTURAL

In areas of high productivity potential and uncertain water availability, major water infrastructure projects are required for increasing water use efficiency through reducing losses, improving water system operations and returning water to the environment.

*Modernizing Irrigation System to Improve Use Efficiency and Increase Water Productivity.* Since 2000, Victoria's government has been investing in modernizing the irrigation distribution systems in northern Victoria. Major investments are also being made to upgrade on-farm works to improve efficiency of water use. In Victoria, the best practice upgrading requires applying laser grading and incorporating reuse systems for large scale gravity irrigation. For higher value crops where sprinkler or micro/drip irrigation is now generally used, farm irrigation systems are designed to apply sufficient water to meet peak water requirements of the target crop. These designs will improve crop yields with the same or reduced amount of water. When sprinklers are used, the average application rate of the sprays should not exceed the soil infiltration rate.

The Northern Sustainable Water Strategy upgraded and modernized Northern Victoria's irrigation network to improve the system distribution efficiency and enhance

---

**Box 4.4: Northern Victoria Irrigation Renewal Project (NVIRP): Modernizing the Goulburn-Murray Irrigation District**

---

NVIRP is the largest irrigation modernization project in Australia and aims to recover 425 GL (or 425 MCM) of water savings from the Goulburn Murray Irrigation District (GMID). Up to 900 GL of water in the GMID has been lost historically through leaks, evaporation and other inefficiencies. The $2 billion investment in NVIRP will increase delivery efficiency in the GMID from about 70% to at least 85%, through physical system upgrading, technological innovations and management enhancement. Most NVIRP water savings will be distributed as new entitlements to the environment, however some of the savings will go to the city of Melbourne and irrigators. In addition to increased efficiency and new entitlements, NVIRP will enable major restructuring of the irrigation system to ensure its sustainability.

*Source:* Graeme Turner, 2012

---

the level of service provided to irrigators by the network as a major initiative in response to on-going water shortage.

The Victoria government, along with other stakeholders, provided funding for three major modernization projects in northern Victoria: (a) the Central Goulburn 1234 Project; (b) the Shepparton Modernization Project and (c) the Northern Victoria Irrigation Renewal Project (NVIRP) (see box 4.4).

The project is to increase the distribution network efficiency by modernizing the network that includes the following works:

- Installing an integrated open channel irrigation control system incorporating automated control gates to better manage supply by accurate flow measurement and control, coupled with software to manage real-time system demand;
- Rationalizing and providing new irrigator supply point metering incorporating automatic control and real-time monitoring to accurately measure and control water onto the farm;
- Channeling bank and bed remedial works incorporating use of plastic lining; and
- Rationalizing channel sections and redundant infrastructure, and replacing existing farm connections with, for example, piped systems to replace open channel systems.

RESULTS

The (Australian) National Water Commission assessed the progress of water planning practice across Australia (NWC 2011c). For northern Victoria, the assessment results are as follows:

- Unprecedented dry conditions between 1997 and 2010 and the recognition of the potential future impacts of climate change are major drivers to the way water use is planned in (northern) Victoria;

- Regional sustainable water strategies and regional river health Strategies articulated long-term water priorities and the key risks to water resources, particularly with respect to climate change and seasonal variability;

- All water plans (short and long term) have been underpinned by extensive community consultation, stakeholder engagement, and assessments of hydrological, environmental, social and economic factor; and

- All water planning processes allowed for water corporations, catchment management authorities, water users and the broader community to appreciate possible future changes to water availability and better manage their own risks.

The NWC's *Annual Australian Water Markets Report*[2] and the annual *Victorian Water Accounts Report*[3] provide evidence that water trading allows more flexibility to irrigators in their water use and production decisions, helping them respond to droughts and changes in commodity prices, etc. For example, water allocation trading (short-term trading), particularly in northern Victoria, have helped irrigators manage their own risks in relation to extended dry periods, as demonstrated by the volume of water allocations traded during the Millennium Drought period when trade increased by 42 percent (see figure 4.2). For entitlement (permanent) trading, there was a sharp increase over 2005–06 (36 MCM) and 2007–08 (388 MCM), the most severe years of the drought.

During this period of severe water scarcity, both water entitlement (permanent) and allocation (short-term) trading across the northern Victoria allowed for increased productivity through the reallocation of water used for agriculture. For example, in 2008–09 trading in this region increased Australia's GDP by $220 million through reallocating water in the Murray-Darling Basin from upstream to downstream and moving from dairy production to horticulture and nut trees (see figure 4.3). The total production benefits were

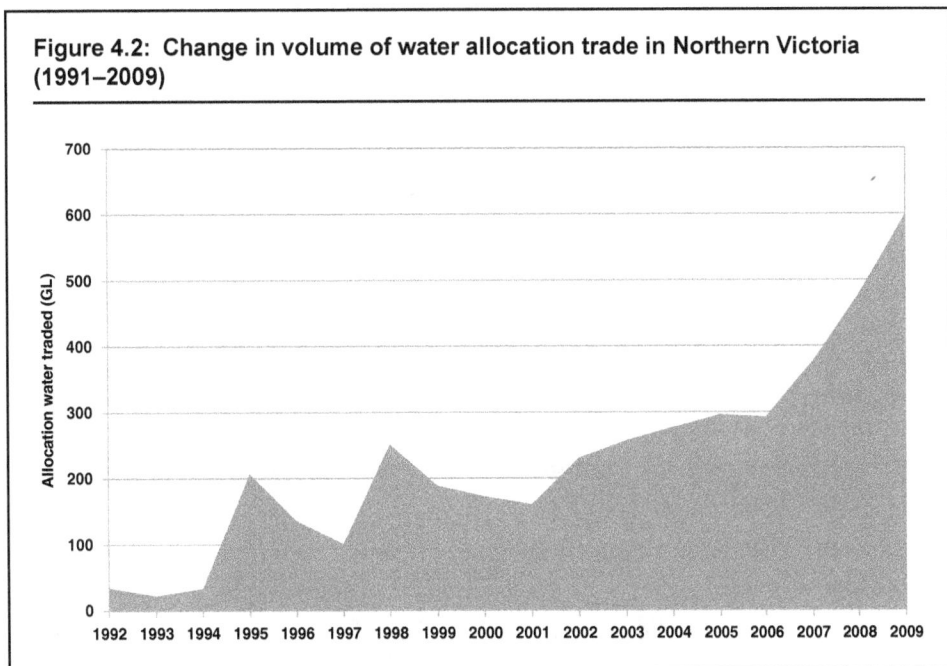

**Figure 4.2: Change in volume of water allocation trade in Northern Victoria (1991–2009)**

*Source:* NWC, 2010

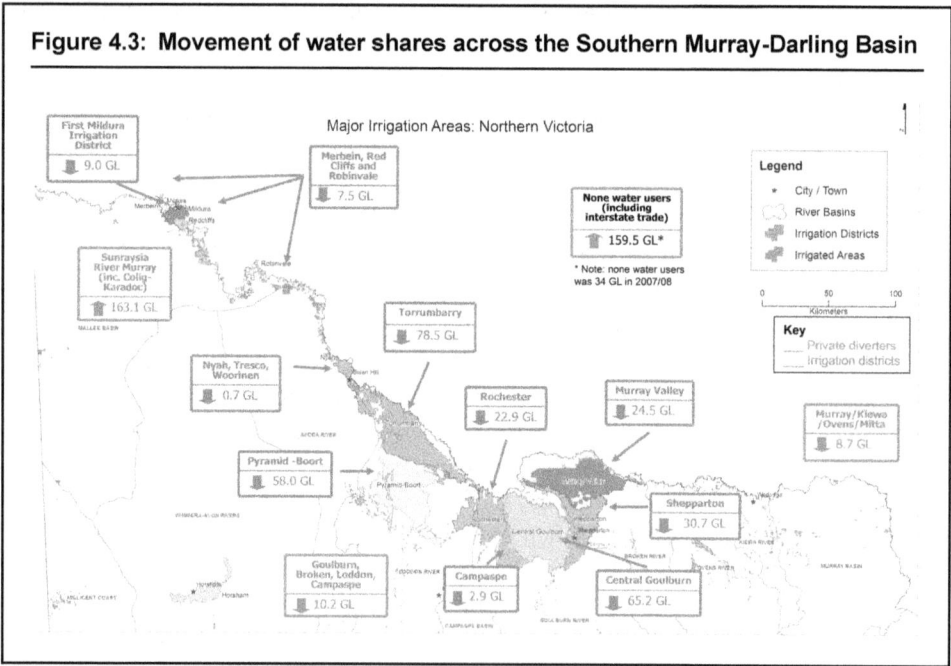

Figure 4.3: Movement of water shares across the Southern Murray-Darling Basin

*Source:* Department of Sustainability and Environment

even greater, at more than $370 million. Other co-benefits were achieved as well by trading water to urban centers and by supporting ecological services (NWC 2010).

Water trading also provided a mechanism for improving flow-related environmental outcomes, even during periods of water scarcity. Major national initiative in the Federal Government's Water for the Future has set aside $A3 billion for purchasing water for the environment to preserve key ecological assets, such as RAMSAR-listed international wetlands, while maintaining the integrity of the existing entitlements framework.

The modernization of irrigation systems, such as the Northern Victorian Irrigation Renewal Project, has resulted in improved distribution efficiencies through reducing losses (e.g., system outfalls, leakage and seepage); more accurate system metering; less deviation in channel supply levels, leading to less channel bank erosion and increased levels of service to gravity irrigators. In northern Victoria, the water distribution network now has several thousand water quality and flow monitoring sites that provide real-time data, displayed and archived at a central server. The amount of data now logged is unprecedented and will provide key inputs into the system operations at all levels. As a result, the system operators are equipped with powerful tools to formally audit the network performance from off-take to the customers' farms. Any problems with performance can be quickly identified and investigated, and unauthorized use or channel leakage promptly rectified (DSE 2010).

### Sydney City: Urban System Level

#### CHALLENGES AND DRIVERS

The Sydney Catchment Authority and Sydney Water Board are responsible for the supply of potable water to the Sydney, Illawarra and Blue Mountain areas. Bulk water is supplied from the authority's system of 18 major dams and two diversion weirs, through a network of pipes and canals to 11 water filtration plants. In the Sydney water service area, the residential sector is the biggest user of water, comprising 61% of total demand. In the 1997 Master Plan the safe yield of Sydney's drinking water storages was estimated as 600MCM/year. The yield is defined as the amount of water that can be withdrawn from a reservoir on a continuous basis with little risk of reducing the reservoir storage to zero. Demand has fluctuated around 600MCM/year since 1980, despite population increase by around 700,000 during the period from 1980 to 1997. However, Sydney's water consumption has been above the safe yield for six of the last ten years up to 2011 (Gunaratnam D. and Li Z. 2010).

A water sector review in 2003 indicated that future water supply security depends on demand management. From 2002–03 onwards, during the drought, the reservoir capacity started to decline, and by 2006, the reservoir capacity dropped to 43.9% of the maximum storage (see figure 4.4). Consequently, it is not feasible to maintain a firm yield of 600 MCM. Efforts in water conservation and demand management must be stepped up.

MANAGEMENT APPROACH: DEMAND MANAGEMENT AND WATER CONSERVATION

To ensure sustainable and reliable water supply for different users, Sydney Water decided to implement, a decade ago, several major water conservation and demand management programs, covering residential, business, water recycling and water leakage reduction. These are briefly summarized below.

*Residential Water Saving Programs*

- **Residential indoor retrofit program.** The *Every Drop Counts* retrofit program started in January 2000, offers households the opportunity to have a plumber visit their house to install water efficient devices;

- **Outdoor water conservation program** — The *Go slow on the $H_2O$* program running since 2000 is an educational program to promote water efficient gardening and other outdoor water use practices;

**Figure 4.4: Fluctuating reservoir storage in Sydney during the past decade (1998–2010)**

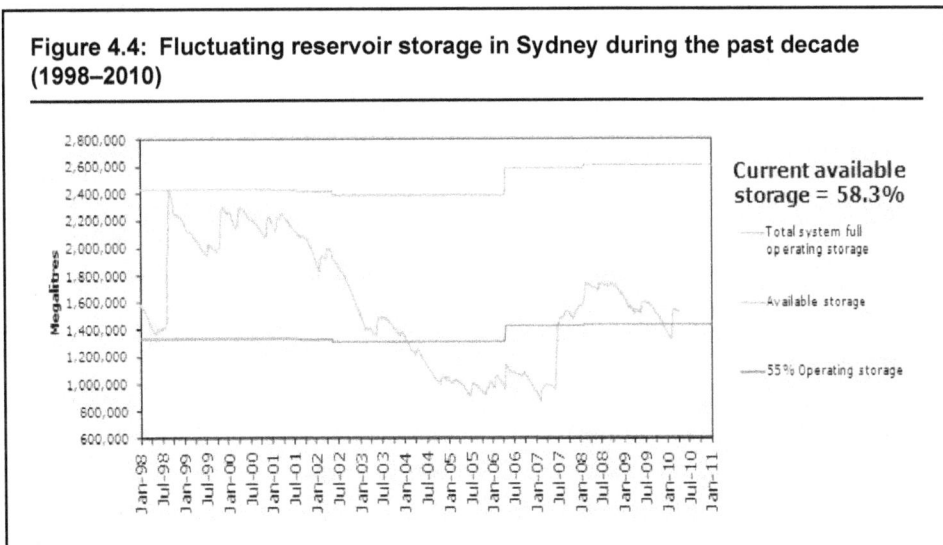

*Source:* Gunaratnam D. and Li Z., 2010

- **Rainwater tank rebate program.** The rebate program assessed whether a rebate incentive stimulates an increase in tank installations and encouraged tank purchasers to install larger size tanks and to connect them to either their toilets or washing machines to utilize rainwater;
- **Water efficient washing machine rebate program.** The program provided a $100 rebate in its early stages to new purchasers of water-efficient washing machines;
- **Public housing retrofit program.** Currently the Department of Housing pays the full cost of public housing tenants' water accounts. Sydney Water and the Department of Housing are discussing an agreement to retrofit Department of Housing properties with water saving facilities; and
- **Residential landscape assessment program.** This program, under development, will provide a garden tune-up and advisory service that targets Sydney's highest outdoor water consumers.

### Business Water Saving Program

The *Every Drop Counts* business program targets customers in the manufacturing, commercial, hospitality, education and government sectors. It focuses on potential participants from the highest water using business sectors and individual water users. The business community embraced the program; about 35% of the business sectors in 2003 formally joined the *Every Drop Counts* business program. In 2009 the business community saved some 22 MCM/yr through these programs, leading to a 15% reduction in water consumption of existing businesses.

### Water Recycling Program

In 1999 Sydney Water developed a Water Recycling Strategy and provided a Water Recycling Projection for 2000–2005. The projection indicated that the volume of water recycled from the sewerage system would increase by between 4 ML/day and 67 ML/day in the future. Sydney developed a Recycled Water Program, indicating which recycled products would be provided to which markets and the delivery schedule over the next ten years. Since 2001, recycled water use has increased from 10 ML/day to 25 ML/day.

### Nonrevenue Water Reduction Program

Sydney Water's active leak detection and repair program is the largest and most comprehensive program in Australia to reduce leakage from its system. As a result, Sydney Water has successfully reduced the non revenue water loss rate from 10.7 percent in 1999 to 7.5 percent in 2009. Their Water Pressure Management program targets those areas where pressure levels are well above average and where there is a history of water main breaks. The program is an important part of Sydney Water's leak prevention program and the New South Wales State Government's Metropolitan Water plan.

### Water Pricing Program

Water pricing in Sydney comprised a number of components. The key features of the water pricing program include: (a) two-part tariffs, incorporating a fixed component and a component that varies with usage; (b) cost based pricing—linking prices paid by customers to the cost of service delivery; (c) removal of cross-subsidies between different customer groups and types of services; (d) removal of property value based charges in favor of user based charges for all services and (e) removal of all pre-paid water allowances.

**Figure 4.5: Demand management impact on reducing total demand**

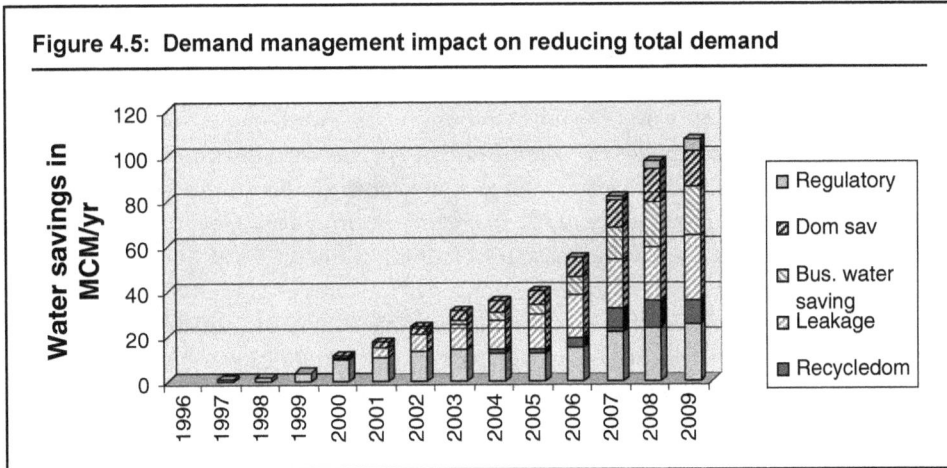

*Source:* Gunaratnam D. and Li Z., 2010

RESULTS

Figure 4.5 shows the total water demand reduction due to water conservation and demand management programs over the years in the city. Annual water use reduction reached 107 MCM by 2009, resulting in a substantial drop in withdrawal rate of water supply reservoir storage from 98% in 2000 to 81% in 2009. Similarly, total water savings increased from 2% of the water demand in 2000 to 18% in 2009. Major water savings were: 26% from leakage reduction, 23% from industrial recycling, 21% from businesses engaging in *Every Drop Counts* program, 15% from residential programs for use of smaller toilet cisterns, water saving shower heads, etc, 10% from recycling grey water in residences and 5% from tariff increases.

*Lessons Learned*

Overall, the northern Victoria case study highlights the importance of *establishing clearly defined water rights; implementing an effective, transparent trading system and modernizing water infrastructure as fundamental steps for managing scarce resources.* Undertaking these steps requires, at national and state government levels, improving communications and stakeholder awareness and participation in management decisions. In particular, government agencies roles and responsibilities in the implementation of agreed plans and management decisions must be defined and made transparent, to increase accountability and confidence that the agreed process will be implemented successfully. Improving the integration and coordination between agencies, including information (e.g., technical, policy and community) sharing is also fundamental to respond effectively to both expected and unexpected changes in water availability.

The unprecedented nature of the recent drought (Millennium Drought) in southeast Australia, particularly its length and severity, *has motivated and accelerated a series of responses to improve water scarcity management, ranging from major policy and planning initiatives (e.g., regional sustainable water strategies) to infrastructure upgrades and system management improvement.*

The Millennium Drought demonstrated to water managers that *climate is not a stationary entity on which planning and system design can be based.* While unplanned contingencies were necessary to respond to the unprecedented conditions, the experience of managing through the drought served to reinforce the relevance of Victoria's water entitlement and planning frameworks and principles which emphasized the need for establishing certainty and flexibility around water entitlements and management.

This approach recognizes that *stakeholders, such as irrigators, urban water corporations and environmental water managers, are generally best placed to manage their own risks under the constraints of the operating environment.* Government is responsible for maintaining the entitlement and planning frameworks at the State level, and managing the residual risk of long-term changes in water availability through reviews and planning processes, each with clear timeframes for periodic update.

*Secure water entitlements and a transparent water trading system are core elements for managing water variability. Secure entitlements provide certainty and clarity regarding responsibility for actions under a range of conditions,* which in turn is supported by: (a) infrastructure to enable water to be delivered where and when required, particularly during drought; (b) placing limits on shorter term and yearly use under entitlements; (c) annual allocations that reference entitlements and entitlement-sharing principles as defined in the Act and bulk entitlements and (d) trade and carryover rules for entitlement holders, allowing individuals to adjust to emerging drought in a manner that best suits them.

*In regards to Victoria's water trading system, transaction costs and time lags in processing applications for trade have created barriers to efficient trade of water to its highest value use.* These issues continue to be addressed by improvements in processing times, particularly with ongoing refinements to the Victorian Water Register. Artificial restrictions on water trade out of irrigation zones, in response to concerns that a rapid exit of irrigators from a given area may have adverse social and economic impacts, also limited the benefits of trading for individuals and created uncertainty for potential buyers and sellers[4]. As such, both Commonwealth and Victorian governments agreed to begin phasing out Victoria's 4 percent limit on inter-district permanent trade, with a view to removing the limit entirely by 2014.

Although the population endured significant hardship during the Millennium Drought, and particularly between 2006 and 2009, they now face very positive outcomes that will enable sustainable management of scarce water resources in future. These outcomes are being delivered through:

- Amendments to entitlements to incorporate sharing arrangements for extreme dry conditions;
- Development of clear and effective regulation of entitlements to ensure continual security of rights;
- Clearer entitlements for the environment and more efficient use of environmental water;
- Reserve rules that reduce the likelihood of years with zero annual allocations;
- Improved flexibility and options through measures such as trade and carryover;
- Streamlining water trading options to enable water to move from low to high value uses;
- Increased use of new and alternative water sources; and
- Modernized and reconfigured irrigation systems.

Further, the government recognized the *need for increased communication and collaboration between authorities responsible for different aspects of water manage-*

*ment to successfully manage a drought.* The Victorian experience resulted in improved understanding of each other's needs, priorities and operations, including infrastructure upgrades to improve efficiency of supply.

The uncertainty surrounding future conditions means that *planning needs to be based on a wide range of plausible future climate scenarios.* New guidelines for the development of urban water management strategies emphasize scenario planning and adaptive management to ensure urban water supply security in the medium to long term. The regional sustainable water strategies were developed during the driest period in Victoria's history, and provided a mechanism for communities to be involved in decisions regarding the best way to secure the region's water in the face of future uncertainty.

In Sydney, coping with water shortage calls for both supply and demand management measures. *Non-structural measures such as water conservation and demand management are very cost-effective investments in bridging the supply-demand gaps and enhancing water security. Most significant contributions to reduction in urban water demand can be made from water supply system leakage reduction, industrial water recycling and reclamation, business and residential water saving programs.* Although water conservation is the common task of all users, diverse programs for different user groups have proved to be very important.

## Israel: National Level

### Challenges and Drivers

Israel is a semi-arid country; population increase coupled with continued economic growth has placed enormous pressure on the country's scarce water resources. Total annual fresh water available in Israel is about 1,800 million cubic meters (MCM) or less than 300 cubic meters per capita. In 2005, approximately 45% of this water was used for municipal consumption (primarily residential), and 50% for agriculture. About 80% of the water potential is in the north of the country and 20% in the south. Normally, water supply fluctuates from year to year depending on the annual rainfall. Groundwater provides 55–70% of the total water supply, determined by the prevailing climatic and hydrological conditions. Israel's main freshwater resources are stored in one lake and two aquifers. The lake and aquifers provide about 80% of the country's fresh water; other smaller water bodies provide the remaining 20%. Increasing water scarcity and use competition are the main drivers for change.

### Management Approach: Productivity-Focused Water Resources Management

The Israeli State owns all water and exercises very tight control on water use. Israel's primary water management legislation, the Water Law of 1959 requires licensing and allocation of all water use (e.g., no riparian or domestic use exemptions). Israeli water legislation emphasizes the following: (a) Water resources are public property, and every person has a right to use water; (b) Available water is distributed according to a prioritization process; (c) Centralized control ensures optimal usage of the limited resource and (d) Representative mechanisms for users influence the allocation rules (World Bank 2006).

Ideally, the water allocation process should follow a priority order of domestic, industrial and agricultural uses. However, actual implementation of allocation favors agricultural use over domestic and industrial uses due to the impact of special interest groups on management decisions. At the distribution level, the national state-owned water company Mekorot, has been very successful in building the national distribution system and in developing partnerships with agricultural users. The result is highly efficient drip and trickle irrigation systems with minimum losses. Local authorities are responsible for water distribution within urban areas.

To ensure sustainable development and water security, Israel has made enormous efforts to improve water resources management. The rigorous enforcement of policy, strategic approach and financial measures has enabled effective management of the nation's scarce water resources and high water productivity, and made the country a world leader in many aspects of water resource management. The following represents the key elements of Israel's water resources management strategy (World Bank 2006 and Graeme Turner 2012).

The key technical (or structural) strategies and measures are:

- **Irrigation technology improvement.** Micro irrigation techniques (figure 4.6 left) enable Israel to increase agricultural productivity twelve fold while limiting agricultural water consumption at around the 1975 level. In addition, Israeli-designed greenhouse systems (figure 4.6 right), including specialized plastic films and heating, ventilation and structure systems, enable farmers to grow more than 3 million roses and 300 tons of tomatoes per hectare per season, which are four times the yields of open fields;

- **Urban demand management.** Through infrastructure renewal and wide use of water efficient appliances, urban water consumption remains largely unchanged over the past 40 years while the population almost doubled and the GDP increased 300%;

- **Use of reclaimed water.** Replacing freshwater supply for agriculture with treated wastewater effluent has been very effective; now 50% of Israel's irrigation is with treated effluent;

- **The National Carrier.** This infrastructure system provided the flexibility to move water from water surplus north to water deficit south; and

- **Desalination.** The desalinization program and water reclamation are the major channels for Israel to increase available water resources.

**Figure 4.6: Irrigation technology improvement in Israel: micro-irrigation (left) and green house (right)**

*Source:* The Israel Project, 2011

The key nonstructural strategies and measures applied in Israel are:

- **Water rights and licensing.** The State ownership of all water rights and the requirement for all water uses to be allocated and licensed are at the core of Israeli water management;

- **Water rationing.** The Water Regulations (Water Use in a Rationing Area) describe priorities in water allocation in rationing areas (geographic areas in which the demand exceeds the supply) in the following order: (a) domestic uses; (b) industrial uses; (c) agricultural uses and (d) other uses. In addition, a quota system restricts the amount of water allocated to different sectors;

- **Irrigation and urban water conservation.** In recognizing the much higher efficiency of drip irrigation and micro-sprinkling irrigation than furrow irrigation (in Israel it is about 90% compared with 64%), Israel has overtime made a major technological shift in irrigation practices. Users have widely adopted water saving measures such as water metering, pipe replacement, electronic monitoring and retrofitting for the urban use sector and have also vigorously promoted water saving devices such as water-efficient toilet flushing, basins and upgrading of taps and showers;

- **Reclaimed wastewater effluents as alternative water source.** Treated domestic effluents, estimated at 400 MCM, form the largest potential water source. Currently, about 250 MCM of such effluents, treated to varying degrees, are utilized for irrigation. The rest is discharged into waterways and the sea due to lack of treatment and reuse facilities; and

- **Runoff interception and artificial recharge.** Water schemes divert storm flow from the rivers into surface reservoirs from which it is pumped into the supply system, or dispersed on spreading grounds and left to percolate into the underground aquifer (mainly along the coastal plain). At present, approximately 40 MCM out of a potential of 135 MCM of storm water are intercepted annually.

- The current agricultural legislation regulates almost all aspects of agricultural production, including land administration, water use and allocation, drainage management, plant protection, veterinary services, production and marketing boards, exemption from the antitrust law, the encouragement of capital investments, etc. It provides the legal basis for regulating the agricultural land and water use for multiple benefits; and

- Agricultural policy is formulated jointly by departments within Ministry of Agriculture and Rural Development, although the Planning Authority is the main department responsible for policy design. Other organizations involved in agricultural policy formulation and implementation coordination include: the Ministry of Finance, the Water Authority, the Ministry of Environmental Protection, the Ministry of Trade, Labor and Industry, etc. These institutions effectively enforce the policy to achieve high agricultural water productivity and farm income.

ECONOMIC AND FINANCING INSTRUMENTS

- **Water pricing.** Water prices are updated from time to time according to changes in the consumer price index, power tariff and the average wage index, to encourage efficient water usage. Also, the water prices are differentiated between user sectors: domestic, industry and agriculture;

- **Water trading.** The government has recently approved a change in the water code enabling holders of water allocations to sell their permanent or timed allocations to others by transferring via the National Water Carrier, thus opening the sector for a market-based trading operation;

- **Private sector participation.** Introduction of market-oriented water pricing has increased private sector involvement in the production and supply of water to various consumers. Consequently, more rational water use can be expected through introducing new water suppliers and more competition;

- **Extraction levies and grants.** Since 1999, an extraction levy has been charged. This levy reflects the scarcity value of the water rather than the cost of extraction. In order to improve water use efficiency, the government provides grants from the State budget to private extractors for development of inferior quality water sources and for conversion into higher quality supply sources;

- **Financial support.** The government also provides grants and low-interest loans for upgrading and expanding water supply and wastewater treatment plants; and

- **Insurance schemes.** Farmers receive government support to participate in an insurance scheme against natural disasters and in a broader multi-risk insurance scheme. Farmers receive partial compensation of the premiums: 80% of the premium to participate in the multi-risk insurance scheme and 35% of the premium to participate in the insurance scheme against natural disasters.

*Results*

Israel's success with water management demonstrates high water use efficiency and productivity, especially in the agricultural sector, and sustainable socio-economic growth in spite of the physical water scarcity:

- The Israeli government has been highly successful in addressing the water scarcity problem, while maintaining a steady rate of economic growth and accommodating the demand of an increasing population. It established well defined water allocation and rights system to enable efficient distribution of water via the national distribution system to the three main user sectors—municipal, agriculture and industry;

- Over the years, the agricultural water use has decreased and diversified substantially. In 1990 freshwater accounted for about 95% of water used by agriculture. This percentage dropped to 55% by 2001 and to 45% by 2008. Around one-third of water used by agriculture now is from reclaimed wastewater effluents, with a further one-fifth from brackish (saline) water. Brackish water is used for irrigation of salinity-tolerant crops like cotton;

- They have achieved high agricultural water productivity through preferential policies, technological transformation and cropping pattern change moving to higher value crops, reducing average requirement for water per unit of land from 8,700 m$^3$ per hectare in 1975 to some 5,500 m$^3$ today. In the meantime, the country saw a 2.2% annual average growth rate of agricultural production over the period of 1990–2008 which is higher than most OECD countries; and

■ The results of urban water conservation and demand management can be seen from the fact that per capita urban water consumption in Israel has hardly changed in the past 40 years while the country has seen an increase of its GDP by 300 percent during the same period.

*Lessons Learned*

The main lessons learned from the Israeli case are:

■ *The very fine balance that exists between available water and increasing demand requires a strictly managed water resource allocation and distribution system.* This system operates at a very high level of efficiency for all use sectors—municipal, industry and agriculture;

■ *Managing water scarcity successfully requires a portfolio of measures,* ranging from a clear strategy, complete legal framework (incl. clear ownership of water), supporting policy and regulations (institutions), to appropriate economic and financial instruments, technological innovations and to targeted investments (e.g., water conservation and productivity improvement programs targeting main users);

■ *Increase in water productivity is the combined effect of many factors.* In Israel, the increase in agricultural water productivity can be attributed to the supporting government policy, advances in irrigation technology, changes in cropping pattern, the skilled Israeli farmers and their ability to adopt innovative technologies and best management practices (MARD 2009); and

■ *Incentive policies and economic instruments stimulate and enable different use sectors to engage in rigorous water conservation* through diversifying water sources, technological innovations and adoption of good management practices, most obviously in irrigated agriculture but also in manufacturing and urban water uses.

## Spain: River Basin Level

*Challenges and Drivers*

Spain, in a Mediterranean climate characterized by recurrent droughts of variable scale and intensity, faces major challenges in meeting the needs of water services of different sectors. High level of urbanization and industrialization puts increasing pressure on the limited water resources available, and requires an integrated approach to managing the competing water demands of different user groups. Various water issues such as frequent droughts (especially in recent years), unmet water demands and environmental degradation, and increasing climate risks, call for a major shift in the management strategy and practices concerning both water quantity and quality.

Following the extreme drought experienced in the past years, the Spanish Government established an Office for Climate Change, and most regional governments have also created climate change groups or divisions which have strong links to water management agencies at corresponding levels.

*Management Approach: Integrated River Basin Management (IRBM)*

Spain probably has the longest history of any country in developing formal government water authorities at the river basin scale (Blomquist et al. 2005). The country is divided into thirteen "Management River Basins" (MRBs), each bringing together several natural river basins for management rationalization and cost-effectiveness consideration. Each MRB has a CH (Confederaciones Hidrográficas) as a basin water authority with a strong stakeholder oversight mechanism, which adopts an integrated, decentralized and participatory approach to management of the basin in line with the requirements of sustainability and efficiency. At the water system (urban and agricultural) level, water is managed by water authorities jointly with Water User Associations (WUAs).

The functions of CH include assigning water concessions and other water administration activities; study, design, construction, and operation of the multi-sector water use infrastructure; hydrologic planning and setting regulatory fees and tariffs based on criteria of rational water use, equitable distribution of responsibilities and benefits among different water users and the level of self-financing of the services. The effective functioning of CHs has enabled the practice of integrated water resources management at the basin level. Such a practice or integrated river basin management (IRBM) promotes the coordinated development and management of water, land and related resources to maximize the resultant socio-economic and environment benefits in an equitable and sustainable manner.

*Featured Measures of the IRBM*

Some of the key measures of the integrated river basin management as practiced in Spain are described as follows:

- **Integrated and participatory management approach.** Both at river basin and water system levels, water resources planning and management are carried out in an integrated and participatory manner by basin authorities and water authorities with involvements of multiple stakeholders (cross-sector and jurisdictions) and water users;
- **Irrigation system modernization and water source diversification.** Irrigation accounts for 58 percent of the total water consumption in the country. Different modernization measures aimed at improving agricultural water use efficiency and agricultural productivity and reducing water consumption have been adopted, such as replacement of flood irrigation with drip and sprinkler irrigation, adjustment of cropping pattern, and making use of alternative water, etc;
- **Water conservation and demand management.** Spanish water law emphasizes the management of demand, encapsulated in the 2001 National Hydrological Plan (NHP) which aims to "manage water rationally, sustainably, sensibly and equitably." The NHP requires all river basin agencies to develop Drought Management Plans, and cities of over 20,000 populations to develop Drought Emergency Plans (Velez et al. 2011). Spain's water utilities devote much attention to water conservation and water demand management in addressing water scarcity issues, and increasing water system resiliency and have adopted various innovative measures over the years. These include: conjunctive use of surface water and groundwater, restriction on the use of portable water in agriculture, installation of household water meter, non-revenue water reduction (in particular loss reduction from water distribution network), installation of a separate network for non-drinkable water, water pricing and incentive-based water tariff program, etc;
- **Virtual water trade.** Spain imports water-intensive crops of low-economic value (mainly wheat, maize and soybeans) and exports water-efficient high economic

value commodities grown well in the Mediterranean climate (e.g., olive oil, fruits and vegetables). This approach of virtual water import helps preserve the scarce water resources and ease water shortage situation; and

▨ **Advanced monitoring and management information system.** Spain has established an advanced hydrological information system for real time data management (level of reservoirs, state of main water control gates and discharge at control points) at the basin level. Such information system enables credible prediction over water availability and water flows, to alert decision makers and stakeholders of alarming water conditions, and supports effective decision making and management control in water resources management.

*Results*

Results of the integrated approach to water resources management in Spain have been very positive and promising. Some of the key outcomes are summarized below:

▨ The country established a strong institutional framework for integrated basin management and water management at different levels, and for dealing with climate change and adaptation. Central to this effective framework is the devolution of responsibilities for the important planning and management decisions down to the local level with clear national and basin level guidance;

▨ The drought experience has helped build a culture of water conservation among the communities, which the water authorities strive to maintain through outreach campaigns. The participatory and decentralized approach adopted in the water sector of Spain has also proved valuable;

▨ Cost-effective GWD measures, including technological upgrading for water conservation and diversification of water sources (treated wastewater, rainwater harvesting, etc) for big water users, have enabled substantial freshwater savings in water stressed basins, particularly in the agricultural sector (see figure 4.7);

**Figure 4.7: Annual freshwater withdrawals for agriculture (percentage of total withdrawal) in Spain**

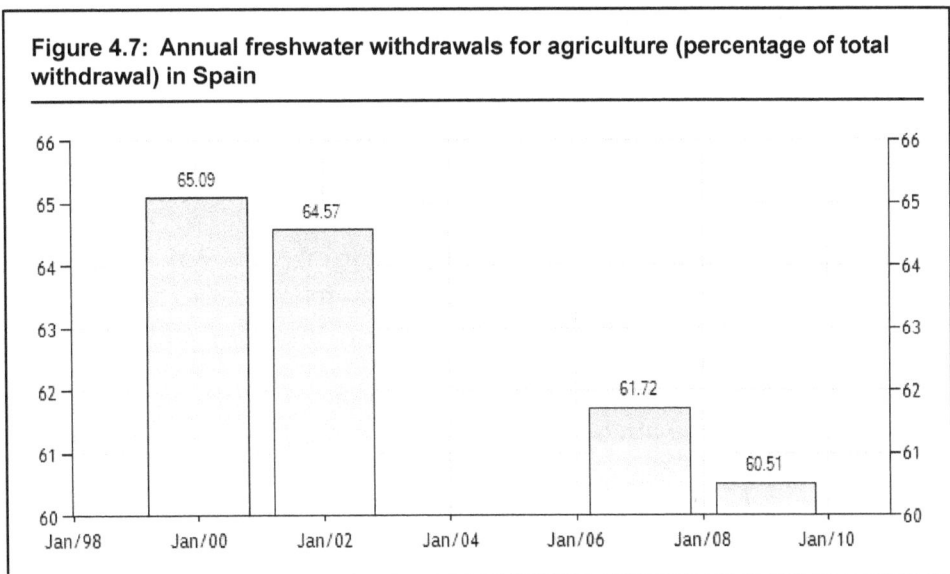

*Source:* www.tradingeconomics.com/spain.

- Water-savings were accompanied by significant energy saving and GHG emission reduction. For example, from 2006 to 2010, Canal Isabel II was able to save 483 million $m^3$ of water, equal to 409 GWH of energy and 213.5 KT of carbon dioxide;

- Investments in modernizing the water supply and sanitation system resulted in approximately 70 $hm^3$ of water saved per year, the equivalent of 18.1% of total consumption in Alagon city. Similarly, demand management initiatives led to city wide reduction in per capita water consumption, particularly during dry periods; and

- As a result of virtual water trade, Spain 'imported' about 27 $km^3$/year and "exported" 17 $km^3$/year through agricultural product trade, resulting in a negative balance of 10 $km^3$/year (equivalent to a net-water saving of 10 $km^3$/year for Spain).

### Lessons Learned

Based on the literature reviewed, some of the most important lessons of the Spanish experiences learned are as follows:

- *A participatory approach through a multi-stakeholder organization is indispensable for integrated river basin management and agricultural water management* to ensure integrated planning, equitable water allocation, accountability in system performance and sustainable water development. Water users who share the same intake or concession management unit, are required by law to establish WUAs. When water is used for irrigation, these associations are known as irrigation associations (Comunidades de regantes or CRS). Currently there are some 6,200 CRS in Spain. These are nonprofit associations of all the landowners in irrigated areas that are required by law to autonomously and collectively administer public waters;

- *Public and private partnership play a pivotal role in introducing market mechanisms for water supply and sanitation services and in conserving water in the urban areas.* According to the Spanish Water Supply and Sanitation association (AEAS), as cited by Ortega and Pizarro (2008), 40% of the population receives water supplied by public utilities, 36% from private companies, 16% from public-private partnership entities and about 7% from the local governments;

- *Effective demand management measures serve the urban water sector well in significantly reducing water consumption.* Such measures include block water tariffs, incentives policies and subsidy programs for water conservation, etc;

- *Virtual water trade proved to be an effective strategy in reducing agricultural water consumption and mitigating water shortage at the country or local government levels;*

- *Through addressing the water-energy use linkage, water utilities can minimize environmental impact and reduce operating costs.* The drive for energy self sufficiency and green growth in major cities can also benefit from this practice; and

- *Sustainable water resources management at different levels benefit enormously from a strong water conservation culture* which commands active support from water user communities and the general public to water saving initiatives and climate change adaptation.

## Northern China: River Basin, Local Government and Irrigation System Levels

*Challenges and Drivers*

China, with an annual per capita freshwater resource of around 2,160 m$^3$, is a water-stressed country. The uneven spatial and temporal distribution of water resources further increases the severity of the problem. Water availability in different parts of China varies greatly due to characteristics of its climate and topography. This spatial disparity does not match the distribution of China's population, arable land, and productivity. In northern China, the region with highest level of water scarcity, water shortage is becoming a major constraint to sustainable development. In many areas of the north, increasing water demand in different use sectors has led to over-exploitation of available water resources and eco-environmental degradation, an apparent sign of water scarcity and stress (World Bank 2009).

The impact of climate change further aggravates water scarcity in northern China, e.g., over the past 20 years, mainstream water flows have declined substantially in the 3H basins, namely, Huang (Yellow), Huai and Hai river basins. More specifically, the flow has dropped by 41% in the Hai River basin, 15% in the Yellow river basin and 15% in the Huai river basin. Climate change projections suggest an increasing uncertainty over future precipitation intensity and patterns. Expected higher evaporation, uneven spatial and temporal distribution of precipitation will make the severe water scarcity situation in northern China even worse. For the 3H basins, the current water shortage of about 30–40 km$^3$ per year (30,000–40,000 GL) is projected to rise to 56.5 km$^3$ by 2050. Unless effective measures are taken to substantially save water and reduce demand, water resources in these regions are no longer sustainable (World Bank 2009).

The Yellow River is the second largest river basin in China. It flows through nine provinces and is the major source of water for the Northwest and North of China. Water scarcity in the Yellow River basin has been further compounded by over use of groundwater and the lack of integrated institutional arrangements to deal with the problem. The Hai River basin is even more water scarce. Located in the North China Plain, it covers four provinces and two province-level municipalities (Beijing and Tianjin). It is characterized by semi-arid climate with 400–500mm annual average precipitation, substantial water resources deficiency, wide-spread water pollution and severe groundwater overdraft, as a result of rapid economic growth and urbanization, etc. This study uses Ningxia Hui Autonomous Region (Province), located in the upper reach of the Yellow River basin, and a groundwater irrigated area in Guantao County of Hebei Province within Hai River basin, as cases, to illustrate the emerging best practices in China.

*Ningxia Region.* In the Yellow river basin, the total available water resources have substantially decreased in the past decades, particularly during the consecutive drought years. According to recent water resources assessments for Ningxia, the average annual precipitation in the past decade has decreased by about 10–15% comparing with the average of the complete historical data series; the maximum water diversion from the Yellow River allocated to Ningxia fell by 4% from the past 6.74 billion m$^3$ (6,740 GL) to the current 6.47 billion m$^3$ (6,470 GL) because of the decreased water inflow in the basin (World Bank 2009).

The low water use efficiency in irrigation has been a long standing issue. In Ningxia and most other provinces in northern China many of the irrigation systems were built 30–40 years ago with substandard designs and incomplete on-farm systems; most have further deteriorated due to deferred maintenance, resulting in very low water use efficiency. Despite the government's enormous investments in renovating the large and medium irrigation schemes over past decades, many of them are still in needs of upgrading to improve water use efficiency and productivity. The efficiency of irrigation water use is about 40% in Ningxia on average as a result of serious water seepage from aged or incomplete main canal systems, unlined on-farm canals and ditches and flood irrigation with significant amount of water lost through Non-Beneficial Evapo-Transpiration (NBET) in the dry climate (World Bank 2009).

The decreasing trend of water availability in the basin and province and pressing needs for increasing water use efficiency and productivity in all use sectors, particularly the agricultural sector, are the main drivers for Ningxia to change its strategy of managing the limited water resources.

*Guantao County.* Located in the water-scarce Hai River basin, Guantao County is an agricultural county which relies mainly on groundwater for irrigation and other uses. Uncontrolled water withdrawal from underground for irrigation in the past by farmers in Guantao and neighboring counties has led to severe groundwater overdraft over the county and beyond. The main water resources issues and drivers for change are summarized below:

- **Major water supply-demand gap and severe groundwater overdraft:** e.g., in the Beigu Village of Guantao County, water use for production and life all depends on groundwater. Actual annual groundwater withdrawal amounts to 0.4 MCM while the safe yield is only 0.1 MCM;
- **High percentage of water-intensive and low-value crops** such as winter wheat (accounting for 60–70 percent of total cultivated area) leads to high water consumption in agriculture and low farm income;
- **Outdated irrigation management and production practices** are reflected in high irrigation quota (about 200–300 mm per crop) and low water use efficiency, low system performance (e.g., water supply reliability) and water charge based on farm size and head counts, etc;
- **Water pollution and environmental degradation:** overuse of chemical fertilizers and pesticides, uncontrolled disposal of human/livestock and solid wastes, and lack of management control over use of brackish groundwater for irrigation, result in groundwater contamination and soil salinization; and
- **There is a general lack of participation of water users in water management decisions and implementation.** Water users are not happy with the irrigation performance and are concerned about the increasing costs of pumping (and stagnant farm income) and level of uncertainty in water availability.

*Management Approach at Different Levels: Water Conservation*
*Society and Productivity-Focused Agricultural Water Savings*

NATIONAL AND RIVER BASIN LEVELS

Over the last two decades, China's water sector saw a gradual transition from construction focused approach towards resources management oriented approach. In 2002, China's Water Law was amended to embrace the idea of integrated water resources management with focus on the following areas: (a) water allocation; (b) water rights and water withdrawal permits; (c) river basin management; (d) water use efficiency and conservation and (e) protecting water resources from pollution.

In response to the complex issues in water resources development and management facing the northern regions, China engaged in a continuous renewal process, and reinstated its general strategy with the National Five-Year Plan and Medium-Term Plan of Water Resources Development. This strategy required enforcement of strict water resources management in all water use sectors of water-scarce regions, particularly in the biggest water use sector—irrigated agriculture, by means of total water balance control, efficient water use and water pollution control, to ensure the sustainable development of water resources. At the same time, the government strongly emphasized the need for integration between agricultural water savings and increases in agricultural production and farm income. More specifically, the national water resources management strategy prescribed the following types of interventions:

- Match economic/industry structure with local water availability; promote 'water-conservation society' building nationwide and invest in water conservation (including water saving, loss reduction, pollution control and recycling & reuse, etc) and demand management in all user sectors, particularly agriculture and industries, to increase water use efficiency and water productivity, and ensure water and eco-environment security;

- Allocate water based on availability and enforce strict total water control and a quota system at the basin and different administrative levels in water stressed regions, in particular the 3H basins;

- Prioritize management measures based on their cost effectiveness in reducing the water demand—supply gap, as illustrated by a recent study (See figure 4.8);

**Figure 4.8: Cost-effectiveness of different measures and their incremental potential for water saving and augmentation**

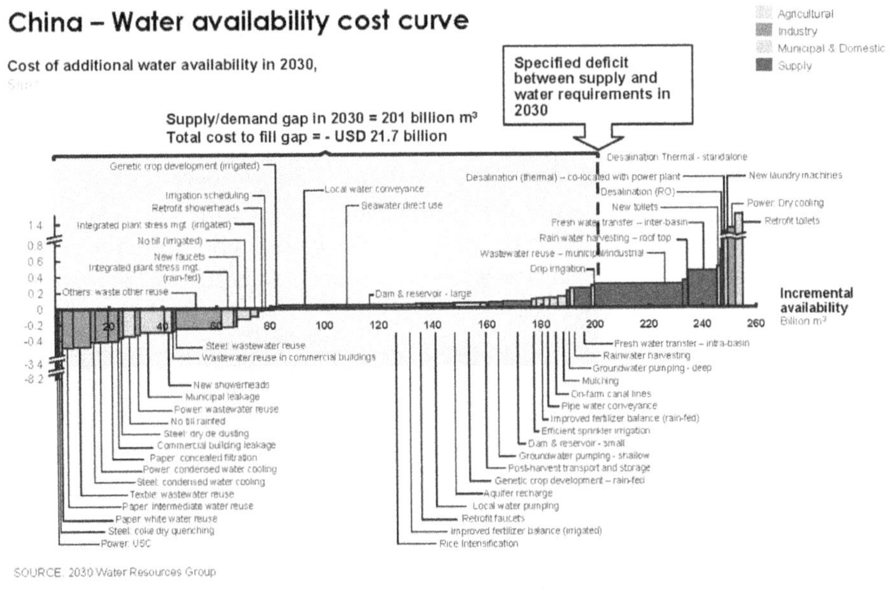

▩ Improve irrigation system performance (in terms of service quality, cost recovery and O&M) by combining physical rehabilitation with institutional reform to make the irrigation service provider more accountable to users, and having users directly involved in irrigation management; and

▩ Increase agricultural production (productivity) and farm income through integrated agronomic, technological and management measures of water saving.

The approach taken at the basin level very much resembles the national one. To deal with the dilemma of increasing demand and limited water resources in the Yellow River Basin, sharing arrangements between the riparian provinces of Yellow River were first agreed upon through a water allocation plan endorsed by the State Council in 1987 and rationalized again in 1998. The Yellow River Conservancy Commission (YRCC) was charged with responsibility of developing an integrated water resources management plan and establishing allocations at the basin scale. The commission also established a system for granting of water use permits (licenses). Within the basin, the provinces and municipalities (cities) formulate their respective strategies in light of the national policy and basin plan.

NINGXIA: PROVINCIAL LEVEL

Ningxia started during the tenth Five-Year Plan period (2001–2005) the planning process for establishing a water-conservation society (Liu, Y. 2012). In 2006, a master plan for building a water-conservation society in Ningxia was endorsed by the national government. The master plan adopted the following principles and key areas of interventions (mostly non-structural) which reflect Ningxia's strategy for water resources management in the province:

▩ **Raise awareness of water users and the public of water scarcity.** It helps to gain support for implementation of the 'water-conservation society' initiative across all sectors in the province;

▩ **Determine production capacity based on available water resources.** The structure and scale of industries and size of irrigated areas (all farmlands are irrigated in Ningxia) as well as cropping patterns must be compatible with the local water resources conditions;

▩ **Improve water allocation through water use right trading.** The intension was to promote fair water use right trading between agriculture, municipalities and industries to optimize the water allocation and improve water productivity;

▩ **Meet high-priority water demand through water conservation.** Water conservation measures are taken in economic sectors to ensure minimum water requirements of ecological services, and reduce domestic and industrial water consumption through rigorous water conservation and productivity improvement with participation of user community (WUAs in the case of irrigation); and

▩ **Use market mechanisms and incentive policies to promote water conservation,** including market tools and incentive policies such as volumetric water pricing, government financial supports to water saving initiatives, "compensation" programs for agricultural and industrial water savings.

Many of the measures highlighted above are implemented across the board, while those more dramatic reform initiatives involved small pilots with limited scope and scale. These measures include: (a) effective water saving technologies: drip and micro-sprinkler irrigation, adapted to the local conditions; (b) water use right trading between an irrigation district and industrial park and (c) a water conservation program targeting water-intensive industries to promote water-efficient technologies and management practices.

BEIGU VILLAGE/GUANTAO COUNTY: IRRIGATION SYSTEM LEVEL

The case of Beigu Village of Guantao County (instead of the County), representative of the county situation, is illustrated here. The management strategy formulated during the Bank supported Water Conservation Project and enhanced under GEF Hai Basin Integrated Water and Environment Management Project, focused on implementing comprehensive agricultural water-conservation measures for real water savings (i.e., ET reduction) and integrating water and environmental management. Different alternatives were compared in consultation with the user communities. For instance, for agricultural water saving measures, three cropping pattern alternatives were discussed with the water user association at the village level: (a) to reduce the area for wheat, maize and increase the area for cotton; (b) to reduce the area for wheat, maize and increase the area for vegetables and (c) to reduce the area for wheat, maize and increase the area for oil seeds and medical herbs. The village agreed to increase the cotton growing area from 35% to 53% while reducing wheat and maize areas, in addition to engineering measures (e.g., adopting piped distribution system) and other measures (ET quota allocation and enforcement and soil moisture preservation, etc).

This integrated water conservation approach has many elements of the GWD concept as it aims to achieve high water productivity through adaptive management, while conserving water and ecological environment and reducing negative impacts. The key features of this management approach adopted in Guantao County covering Beigu Village are as follows:

- **Develop and implement an Integrated Water and Environment Management Plan (IWEMP) and groundwater management action plan for Guantao County:** This plan was based on Guantao's ET allocation (i.e., water consumption quota) set by Hai River Basin Commission and Hebei Province to revert the groundwater overdraft trend;
- **Focus on ET management in line with the total water volume control and quota system:** This plan includes determining the target ET based on the local precipitation and groundwater condition; allocating the ET quota (or water consumption quota) to farm households — as members of WUA — based on the size of their respective cultivated areas; installing water measurement and monitoring devices for groundwater pumping monitoring; using prepaid water use card or intelligent card (IC card) to control groundwater withdrawal; using remote sensing and/or ground monitoring to measure the actual ET and adopting incentive policies (e.g., much higher water tariff rate for over-withdrawal) to encourage water saving;
- **Develop and implement water conservation measures:** For example, on-farm storage of rainwater to reduce need for irrigation; land leveling and creation of smaller farm plots for irrigation; plastic mulching and zero tillage; using drought resistant crop verities and use of low pressure pipeline, drip and micro irrigation. These measures are combined with yield and productivity improvement activities aiming to increase farm income and are supported through government water-saving and/or agricultural development programs with beneficiary contributions;

▩ **Promote participatory irrigation management:** The focus was on establishing and empowering WUAs, which play a very important role in water allocation, consumption monitoring, water saving measures implementation and irrigation system operation and management; and

▩ **Integrate water and environmental conservation measures:** Measures include prohibiting use of pesticide of high toxicity and residuals and promoting use of bio-pesticides that are easy to dissolve and less toxic; adopting balanced fertilizer application practices and increasing use of organic fertilizers to save farmers' investment on fertilizers and reduce negative impact on the water bodies and ecosystem; proper handling and utilization of livestock and human wastes (manures) to reduce groundwater contamination and appropriate use (e.g., mixed with fresh water) of brackish shallow groundwater to prevent soil salinization.

*Results*

*Ningxia Region.* In the past five years, Ningxia has witnessed a continued socio-economic growth, as well as significant progress in implementing the new water management strategy which is described below.

▩ **An initial water allocation system has been formulated, and a number of initial water right trading pilot projects successfully concluded.** An entitlement system that establishes clear sharing of the available water resources, including shares of the system losses, has been formulated for annual water allocation, transfer and trading. However, this entitlement system has yet to be established legally with clear policy and operational procedures. In the longer term these will be necessary to provide the needed mechanism and incentives to further improve the efficiency of the irrigation systems and achieve higher water productivity;

▩ **As a big step forward in building "water-conservation society," Ningxia has started to rationalize its economic/industrial structure in consideration of the water and other key constraints.** This is evidenced by the significant change in the ratios of three industries (1st~3rd) from 11.0:48.4:40.6 in 2006 to 9.7:50.7:39.6 in 2010;

▩ **Annual water use in Ningxia has seen continued decline in terms of total consumption and irrigation water withdrawal.** As indicated in table 4.1, the GDP of Ningxia grew annually at an average rate of 12.7% from 2005 to 2010 while the total water consumption and irrigation water withdraw from the Yellow River has decreased on a year-to-year basis (Liu, Y. 2012). Of course, one of the reasons for the substantial water savings in Ningxia is because of the rather low use efficiency in irrigation in the first place; and

**Table 4.1: Water consumption in Ningxia, 2005–2010**

| Year | 2005 | 2006 | 2007 | 2008 | 2009 | 2010 |
|---|---|---|---|---|---|---|
| GDP (Billion Yuan) | 612.61 | 725.90 | 919.11 | 1203.92 | 1353.31 | 1643.41 |
| Total Water consumption (billion m³) | 78.08 | 77.63 | 71.00 | 74.18 | 72.23 | 72.37 |
| Irrigation water Withdrawal (billion m³) | 71.87 | 71.72 | 65.07 | 68.38 | 66.29 | 66.08 |

*Source:* Liu, Y. 2012

- Water conservation practices began to take root in different user sectors. Water use efficiency in main use sectors has improved significantly through industrial structure adjustments, technological upgrading and production/management practice improvements for water savings and productivity enhancement. This is reflected in the significant drop in unit water consumption of industrial and agricultural production (See table 4.2 below).

**Table 4.2: Unit water consumption in Ningxia, 2005–2010**

| Year | 2005 | 2006 | 2007 | 2008 | 2009 | 2010 |
|---|---|---|---|---|---|---|
| Water consumption per $10^4$ Yuan GDP ($m^3/10^4$ Yuan) | 1274 | 1124 | 913 | 847 | 737 | 651 |
| Water consumption per $10^4$ Yuan industrial value added ($m^3/10^4$ Yuan) | 151 | 127 | 119 | 90 | 90 | 91 |
| Water consumption per $10^4$ Yuan agricultural value added ($m^3/10^4$ Yuan) | 5376 | 4739 | 4336 | 4081 | 3828 | 3259 |

*Source:* Liu, Y. 2012

*Guantao County.* The results achieved in water conservation and productivity improvement in Guantao County and other counties of Hebei Province, under the Water Conservation Project and GEF Hai Basin Integrated Water and Environment Management Project, are discussed below (World Bank 2007 and 2011):

- Water productivity (the value of agricultural production per unit of water consumed) increased substantially through reduction of non-beneficial water consumption and increase in farm production, resulting in substantial water savings. Production per unit of ET (water consumption) for all crops planted within the project areas increased by 60–80%; agricultural production and farm income both rose by over 100%; the resultant total annual non-beneficial water consumption reduction or real water savings, was equivalent to 123 mm rainfall on average (water consumption reduced from 735 mm to 612 mm). Groundwater monitoring results in Guantao County over the past years, indicated a trend of groundwater level stabilizing with signs of gradual recovery;
- An Integrated Water and Environment Management Plan (IWEMP) with improved knowledge base has been developed, a Groundwater Management Action Plan prepared, and a groundwater management regulation issued by Guantao County with endorsement of the local people's congress. This provided a sound basis for developing and managing Guantao's water resources sustainably;
- Mechanisms for sustainable use and management of water resources were established. A functioning inter-agency committee was established at the county level, with improved coordination and integration of water resources management and pollution control activities; self-managed WUAs were established and empowered for participating in water allocation and irrigation management at the community level; volumetric water charging was operational in all irrigated areas; water consumption (ET) quota was allocated to household level, and a primary monitoring system for groundwater pumping for irrigation, was in place in Guantao County;

*Lessons Learned*

*From the Ningxia Region Case.* The major lessons of experience from the Ningxia case are summarized as follows:

- *The 'building water-conservation society' initiative works well in raising the public and water users' awareness of water scarcity and sense of urgency* to use water efficiently and adapting to uncertain water availability;

- *Support to water use efficiency and productivity improvement through targeted programs is key* to transforming the local economy towards a more water-efficient one and achieving sustainable development in arid and semi-arid areas where water resources are scarce and the ecosystem fragile. The industry structure and production capacity should be made compatible with local water resources availability;

- *Effective water scarcity management calls for the establishment of a water allocation & entitlement system* which allocates water from basin to province to county and water user levels, and provides for mechanism of reallocation and transfer/trading. In Ningxia, this took the form of water use quota and total use control. Apparently a good information base and functional monitoring and enforcement arrangements are essential;

- *Agricultural water use has large potential in water saving which can be realized through a comprehensive package of water-saving measures:* technical, management and agricultural measures, leading to higher crop water productivity. This can be achieved through implementing targeted water-saving programs including demand-side management mechanism such as volumetric water pricing and promotion of crop diversification, and WUA-based participatory irrigation management; and

- *The results from the agriculture-industry water trading pilots through industry supported agricultural water saving interventions are promising in improving water productivity and reducing total water consumption.* These are worthy of further studying for replication and scaling up.

*From the Guantao County Case.* In the case of Guantao County, the key lessons learned in improving scarce water resources management based on the outcomes of the pilot programs under the projects (World Bank 2007 and 2011) include:

- *An ET-based approach to water scarcity management, which targets the reduction in consumptive use or ET, rather than the increase in irrigation efficiency which often results in increases in consumption of water through expansion of effective irrigation areas, proved to be effective. This new approach can lead to real water savings and sustainable water use in physically water-stressed areas.* This practice is being replicated and scaled up at the basin level (Hai Basin) and other arid areas such as Xinjiang autonomous region in China's northwest, where it is being used for overall river basin water resources planning and management, and for allocation of water use and consumption (ET) quotas at all levels from sub-basins down to administrative areas to users. Experiences in northern China show that focusing on improvements to physical infrastructure such as canal lining may increase irrigation efficiency but may also reduce groundwater recharge and increase ET, affecting other uses. Only reduction in actual consumption of water represents genuine savings of water resource in a hydrological system. Based on this approach, target ET (or ET quota) determined by use of remote sensing and modeling analysis can be converted into an allocation quota or a withdrawal limit for the users to control surface water or groundwater abstraction. Water-saving measures can then be designed jointly with user communities to keep water consumption below the limit;

- *A comprehensive water conservation approach giving priority to farmer incentives can achieve multiple-win results:* through a comprehensive approach involving not only engineering works upgrading but also agricultural investments, irrigation management and institution improvement, it is possible to increase farm incomes while reducing water consumption and environmental impacts. Initiatives of agricultural water saving and productivity improvement are more likely to succeed if they give priority to user incentives to change their water use and management behavior. In this respect, well-functioning WUAs proved to be a crucial success factor;

- *Necessary institutional mechanisms and management tools are required to implement integrated water and environmental management:* these include inter-agency coordination and collaboration mechanism at basin/sub-basin and local government levels, shared information/knowledge base and decision-support/planning tools, involvement of key stakeholders in the planning, decision-making and implementation process. They also include a well-conceived and robust integrated water and environment management plan, and an effective monitoring and enforcement arrangement. Particularly important is the empowerment of the WUAs in the case of agricultural water use, enhancing the ownership of water-conservation programs and helping align the interest of farmers in increasing farm income at low cost (of agricultural inputs) with the broader interest of better irrigation performance and water consumption reduction; and

- *It takes time to see the effects of the new approach and change people's behavior:* despite the encouraging outcomes of the innovative management approach under the pilot operations, it will take quite some time to change the mindsets and behaviors of decision makers, water planners and managers and operators (service providers). This involves shifts from withdrawal to consumption control, from a single sector and top-down to an integrated cross-sectoral bottom-up approach. Pilot projects at appropriate level (e.g., county or sub-basin) involving decision makers and key stakeholders including management and technical staff and user groups, are good vehicles to demonstrate the effectiveness and benefits of a new approach.

## Notes

1. The Sustainable Rivers Audit provides a long-term assessment of the condition and health of the 23 river valleys in the Murray-Darling Basin.
2. The Australian Water Market reports can be found at: http://www.nwc.gov.au/publications/bookshop/december-2011/australian-water-markets-report-2010-11
3. The Victorian Water Accounts reports can be found at: http://www.water.vic.gov.au/monitoring/accounts
4. However, there is some evidence that water trading accelerated existing processes of social and economic change in some areas, by providing the financial means for struggling irrigators to exit the industry.

# CHAPTER 5

# General Conclusions and Recommendations

The purposes of this chapter are to draw a number of general conclusions from the study and case analysis and to provide the authors' recommendations for the focus areas in applications of the Green Water Defense (GWD) approach.

## General Conclusions

The GWD is a new approach to water scarcity management in line with the Green Growth principles embraced by many countries and international bodies. It aims to achieve sustainable water services for different use sectors while enhancing the ecological system, through an adaptive management approach with emphasis on increasing water productivity and enabling balanced demand and supply-side management interventions. The GWD approach is promising owing to its multiple-win effects and sustainability focus, as illustrated by the various cases of best practices including some emerging best practices in East Asia. From the case studies, the following general conclusions can be drawn:

- The GWD provides valuable conceptual and practical contributions toward water sector's solution to green growth and sustainable development;
- The GWD approach calls for creation of a water-resilient and efficient society;
- The GWD requires strong stakeholder participation in decision-making, and it requires balanced demand and supply-side management and a blend of market mechanism and government regulation tailored to local circumstances;
- Water, as a valuable natural resource, an ecological service media and a potential risk factor, must be managed in its totality within the water cycle and in an integrated manner with other natural resources (land, environment, etc);
- Water resources (scarcity) management needs to be adaptive, right-based, productivity focused and oriented towards multiple functions (productive, conservation and risk reduction); and
- Some GWD practices in water scarcity management may require a long period of time to take root. Targeted incentive policies and market mechanisms are essential to enable mindset and behavior changes.

## Recommendations for GWD Applications in Water Scarcity Management

Water scarcity can threaten water security and cause shocks to socio-economic development in a country, region or water system. This report provides a menu list of GWD measures along the three spatial layers for dealing with water scarcity situations at different scale levels. The report also provides useful insights from the lessons of experiences gained internationally in managing water shortage, and can serve as a general guide for adaptive water resources management in the future.

The applicability of the GWD measures will depend on the nature and location of the water system, the development priorities, socio-economic circumstances, institutional and infrastructure conditions, etc. Furthermore, applying those measures at different scale levels also means different focus, for example, at the national or a local government level, the high priority should be given to creating a policy and institutional framework for water allocation and use management, land use control and adaptive management financing, as well as on raising public awareness and building a water sensitive and conservation society; at the basin level, the focus should be more on establishing a flexible water allocation and entitlement system, multi-stakeholder decision making mechanism, integrated development and management planning and a solid water management information base and decision-support tools; and at the water system level, total water (or water portfolio) management, alignment of water conservation with productivity improvement interventions, and involvement of user community in planning and management, besides the necessary infrastructure, are critical.

To guide the readers in applying the GWD approach to adaptive water scarcity management, the authors wish to draw special attention to the following aspects:

- Initiatives for raising public awareness of water issues, and 'building a water conservation society' should be promoted by different levels of governments;
- Managing water resources of a basin or jurisdiction requires formulating clear vision and strategy based on solid water accounting and assessment, and adjusting local economy structure based on water and land availability taking into account local socio-economic development trends and climate variability;
- Introducing a water allocation and water entitlement/right system, in which the entitlement/right can be made tradable through market mechanisms (e.g., government regulated water market) or government facilitated transfer/trade, is critical; water right should cover both surface and ground water and be allocated starting from basin level down to different levels of jurisdictions to water user entities (organizations) and to individual users or a self-managed user community groups, where appropriate, in a transparent and participatory manner; water allocation enforced through a water permit/licensing system should ideally specify withdrawal, consumption and return (quantity and quality);
- Much needed are developing incentive policies (e.g., pricing policy, credit support or subsidy program, and payment for ecological services policy, etc. to reward water-conservation initiatives) and institutional mechanisms such as participatory water management planning and multi-stakeholder governance for water use management to stimulate behavior change on the parts of water users and to achieve multiple-win results, e.g., combining water productivity increase with water saving in irrigated agriculture;
- Water suppliers (utilities and irrigation management entities, etc) need support in terms of adaptive water management best practices and technological innovations for enhancing water supply services and water conservation along the water cycle; and
- Also important are promoting the adoption of modern technologies and management tools such as remote sensing, satellite technologies and management control facilities for measuring, evaluating and controlling water use and effects of water-conservation interventions and establishing a decision support system (DSS) for water allocation and use planning and operational management.

# CHAPTER 6

# Building on Best Practices:
# Towards a Roadmap for East Asia

Water scarcity is becoming a major issue in many parts of the world including East Asia. Climate change projections by different studies suggest that rainfall quantity and distribution tend to be more variable and uncertain, with some areas experiencing an increase in annual rainfall and its intensity, whereas other areas, which may already be water-stressed, are likely to suffer from a decline in rainfall. Such changes and variability will test the effectiveness of water resource management systems of different nations in providing secure and sustainable water supply for all users while protecting key environmental assets and the ecological services they provide. This is the essential concern of the GWD approach which emphasizes an adaptive philosophy and integrated management.

The purposes of this chapter are to summarize the essential elements of the GWD concept framework for adaptive water scarcity management, to distill the key lessons of best practices from the case studies, and to provide a general process and practical examples of the GWD application in East Asia Region.

## Essential Elements of Adaptive Water Scarcity Management

Managing water resources sustainably, particularly where water is or is becoming scarce, requires a wide range of cost-effective non-structural and structural measures. These measures must assist water managers and users in adapting to both expected and unexpected changes in water availability. As the risk of water scarcity increases, greater focus should be given to the measures that provide different options to assist water managers, planners and users to find an appropriate response based on their own circumstances. Emphasis on the maintenance of important environmental assets and ecological health is also required to ensure ecological services can continue to support the sustainability of water systems.

Within the overarching Green Water Defense framework, a conceptual framework for water scarcity management sets out the key elements to consider in designing the management strategy and measures. These elements apply to all water supply systems, including large irrigation systems, urban water systems and multiple-purpose water systems which supply water to different sectors. However, the application of specific measures is largely determined by local considerations. Generally speaking, an effective and flexible water management system includes the following essential elements:

**Knowledge Requirements.** The following represent the fundamental knowledge requirements for adaptive water resources (scarcity) management:

- **Establish current status of inputs and trends.** This includes using climate, ecological and socio-economic data to assess supply limits, environmental flow needs and water use values. Long term climate data and climate change projections are also important data requirements;

- **Determine water system boundary.** The boundary should be set at definable physical limits such as catchment, aquifer or river basin limits, which recognize water flow paths and interconnection of definable water resources. If possible, political or administrative boundaries should be assigned a lesser importance;
- **Decide on water availability.** Assessment should be conducted on the available water resources that can be supplied from the water system by modeling the behavior of the water system under a range of climate scenarios;
- **Determine sustainable water use requirements.** Investigations should be undertaken to determine ecological values of a water system, their potential services, and their water regime requirements; and
- **Assess risks to the resources.** The risks to the resources need to be assessed and factored into allocation decision-making processes.

**Management Tools.** The critical non-structural and structural measures required for a GWD approach to water scarcity management are as follows:

- **Water allocation planning.** This involves water accounting, establishing supply reliability requirements and a priority of supply hierarchy between various users (e.g., towns, agriculture, environment and recreation/society), setting a cap and establishing a trade-off process;
- **Water entitlement system.** This is the core mechanism for managing water systems where demand is, or has the potential, to be greater than the supply. It is a prerequisite for the establishment of water markets or trading systems to allow reallocation of water efficiently to higher value uses and to facilitate supply efficiency improvement. Implementing entitlement systems requires accurate measurement of supplies;
- **Publicly accessible water registers.** These are required to record entitlement ownership details, total entitlement volume and seasonal allocation allowed against the entitlement. They are important where water allocation has been capped, and they provide essential information for water managers and for the operation of water markets/trading systems;
- **Economically viable infrastructure.** There are many structural solutions to improve the efficiency of water supply works and water availability. These infrastructure investments must be cost-effective and adapted to the circumstances, as they often involve major expenditure of limited funds, and they should be accompanied by incentives to ensure the works are maintained properly and the improved supply efficiencies are retained;
- **Demand management and water conservation.** They refer to policy and management interventions to curtail water demand, reduce consumption and protect water and related ecological systems; and
- **Augmentation from alternative water sources.** This can involve use of reclaimed and recycled water, brackish water, and rainwater harvesting, etc. for portable and non-portable uses respectively.

## Key Lessons of Best Practices

Examples of the GWD measures and (emerging) best practices in selected countries have been presented in the report. In each case analysis, where scarcity is a major concern, the elements that together fit within the Green Water Defense framework have been, or are under, consideration to varying degree. It is appropriate in all cases that local considerations, including political, socio-economic conditions, determine the emphasis placed on each of these elements and how the individual measures are adapted to local circumstances. For easy reference, the key lessons of best practices from the case studies are summarized below:

- *Water resources management at all levels can benefit enormously from a strong water conservation culture.* Such initiative as 'building a water-conservation society' serves to raise public and water users' awareness of water scarcity and sense of urgency to use water efficiently and increase communities' resilience to climate variability through adapting to uncertain water availability;

- *Managing water scarcity successfully requires a portfolio of measures,* ranging from a clear strategy, strong legal framework (including clear ownership of water), supporting policy and regulations (institutions), appropriate economic and financial instruments, technological innovations, and targeted water management investments (e.g., water conservation initiatives by main users and targeted productivity improvement programs). Maintaining a good balance between very limited water resources available and increasing water demand requires strict management of water allocation and distribution system to ensure that it operates at a high level of efficiency for different uses, as illustrated in the Israeli case. Further, the uncertainty surrounding future conditions means that planning needs to be based on a wide range of plausible future climate scenarios;

- *Improving consumption-based water productivity is at the heart of adaptive water scarcity management.* Improving water productivity is the combined effect of many factors. In Israel, the increase in agricultural water productivity can be attributed to the supportive government policy, advances in irrigation technology, changes in cropping pattern, use of alternative water sources and the skills of Israeli farmers and their ability to adopt innovative technologies and best management practices;

- *Effective water scarcity management calls for establishing a clearly defined and transparent water allocation and entitlement/right system* which allocates water from basin to different levels of governments/water authorities and to water users, and provides for a mechanism of reallocation and transfer/trading, as demonstrated in the Victorian case. Secure entitlements to water and a transparent water trading system are crucial for managing water variability. They provide certainty and clarity regarding responsibility for actions under a range of conditions;

- *Agricultural water use has a large potential in water saving through a comprehensive package of water-saving measures (technical, management and agricultural measures).* This can be realized through targeted water-saving and productivity improvement programs combined with demand-side management mechanisms such as volumetric water pricing and promotion of crop diversification, and WUA-based participatory irrigation management;

- *An ET-based approach to water scarcity management which targets reduction in consumptive use or ET, can lead to real agricultural water savings and effec-*

*tive results in sustaining water use in physically water-stressed areas.* This is in contrast with the traditional irrigation-efficiency focused approach that usually results in increases of water consumption through expansion of effective irrigation areas. The ET-based approach targeting reduction in consumptive water use proved to be effective in the North China Plain for adaptive water scarcity management and increasing water productivity;

■ *A comprehensive water conservation practice aligned with farmers' interests can have multiple-win effects of reducing water consumption and environmental impact and increasing farm incomes.* A comprehensive water approach involving not only engineering works upgrading but also irrigation management and agricultural practice improvements makes possible increasing farm incomes while reducing water consumption and gradually restoring groundwater levels in groundwater irrigated areas. Initiatives of agricultural water saving and productivity improvement are more likely to succeed if they give priority to user/farmer incentives to change water use and management practices;

■ *Through addressing the water-energy use linkage, water utilities can minimize environmental impact and reduce operating costs.* The same principle applies to wastewater management and pumping irrigation and drainage;

■ *Water right trading as illustrated in the case of Victoria, Australia, is very effective in reallocating water to high value use and thus in increasing water productivity.* Similarly, at a lower scale level, the agriculture-industry water trading pilots in northern China through industry-supported agricultural water saving showed promising results in improving water allocation towards high value use and in reducing total water consumption;

■ *Virtual water trade cross countries or regions, as demonstrated by the Spanish case, can be an effective strategy in reducing agricultural water consumption and mitigating water shortage at the country or local government levels;*

■ *Coping with water shortage calls for both demand and supply-side management measures.* Nonstructural measures such as water conservation and demand management are very cost-effective investments in bridging the supply-demand gaps and enhancing water security. Most significant contributions to reduction in urban water demand are from tariff (structure and level) adjustment and technological innovations in industrial, business and residential uses.

■ *Incentive policies and economic instruments can stimulate and enable different use sectors to engage in rigorous water conservation* through diversifying water sources, technological innovations and adoption of good management practices, in irrigated agriculture, and in manufacturing and urban water uses; and

■ *A multi-stakeholder participatory approach is indispensable for effective urban and agricultural water management.* Stakeholders, such as farmer user groups, urban water corporations and environmental water managers, are generally best placed to manage their own risks under the constraints of their operating environment. Good communication and collaboration among different water management authorities responsible for different aspects of water management and stakeholder groups are essential when dealing with water shortage, pollution and droughts, etc.

## General Process Recommended for GWD Applications in East Asia

While the applications of GWD approach in terms of selecting the appropriate GWD strategy and measures are very location specific, the following is intended to provide a guide for the general process of strategy formulation, management measures screening, prioritization and implementation:

- **Establish the knowledge base:** This includes water resources accounting and assessment, water register, water management asset inventory, documentation of management institutions, hydro-met monitoring network, water management information system (preferably with spatial database) and a decision-support system;
- **Map key issues in relation to the key water services at different scales (basin and national/local government scales):** The issue identification must be based on a robust analysis of plausible development (land and water) scenarios factoring in likely climate change and variability, and results of institutional analysis and an infrastructure needs assessment;
- **Formulate strategies at different scale levels with shared vision and objectives for water allocation and consumptive use management:** Use both market mechanism and government regulation with stakeholder (particularly user community) participation;
- **Raise the awareness of the water users and general public of the water (scarcity) issues and nurture a culture of water conservation,** through public campaigns and education initiatives;
- **Establish effective management organizations** with cross-sector coordination and collaboration mechanism for investment planning and decision making;
- **Develop policies and regulations** to promote water-efficient development and water conservation, and stimulate technological and institutional innovations;
- **Identify and assess options of key management measures** (structural and non-structural) under the three spatial layers: land and water use, infrastructure and physical base (ecosystem), to address the issues identified at the target level. Different sets of measures can be formulated and screened in light of their contributions and appropriateness for the specific circumstances;
- **Prioritize the management measures based on their cost effectiveness:** Cost effectiveness analysis taking into account the social and ecological costs and benefits, is the objective criterion for investment prioritization and selection. Lessons of best practices from the case studies could serve as practical references; and
- **Develop and implement action plans based on local endorsements and constraints.** Pilot GWD measures if they involve much uncertainty, before scaling-up or mainstreaming. Targeted government programs, public-private partnership initiatives and water development and management projects, supported by development partners such as the World Bank, Asian Development Bank and bilateral organizations, are good vehicles for piloting and implementing adaptive water management.

## Practical Applications of GWD Approach in East Asia

As noted in the introduction chapter, different drivers increase the risk of water shortages in East Asia. The types of drivers include population and economic growth, urbanization and increased demand for water during the dry seasons due to climate change. The potential impacts of these drivers on limited water supplies are likely to be exacerbated by the lack of established rules for allocating water resources in these countries.

In managing the water scarcity challenges created by the above drivers, the GWD study has used examples of sustainable ways to reduce risks, increase productivity, meet critical human needs and protect the health of river system. More specifically, the GWD approach has focused on the following results:

- Increasing **certainty** of annual water available for use;
- Building in **flexibility** to allow water users to manage their own risks;
- Allowing for the **reallocation** of scarce water supplies to a high value use;
- Increasing **security** of the amount of water a user can take over a period of time; and
- Environmentally **sustainable** water systems.

In implementing the GWD approach, a number of fundamental 'starting' steps will contribute to efficient and sustainable use of scarce water resources. These steps are important in both developed and developing countries where water resources are or potentially scarce or over allocated.

### General Starting Steps for GWD Applications at National and Local Government Levels

STEP 1: STRENGTHEN REGULATION: WATER LAW, NATIONAL POLICY, AND STRATEGIC FRAMEWORKS

The national water law and related regulations for managing water resources must be reviewed and where appropriate revised to ensure they embrace the GWD approach and provide a mandate to facilitate the GWD measures. Both national policy (specific principles) and national strategic frameworks (steps to implement the specific principles) should also be reviewed and aligned with the corresponding lower level government frameworks. Incorporating GWD principles into regulation will assist an increase in both the private and public sectors' understanding and thus confidence in, the benefits of applying GWD approach, and how they can be successfully implemented. Beyond regulations, further explanatory notes, guidelines, public communication documents will assist the broader public understanding of water resources management, particularly during dry periods.

Beyond relevant regulations, key elements to be introduced (or where they already exist, reviewed and strengthened) are the establishment of water rights and water sharing plan frameworks, a water rights trading and register system where circumstances allows, the rules for protecting environmental flow requirements, the establishment of river basin organizations, water sector financing principles and clarification of water ministry's roles and responsibilities (See Step 3). These need to incorporate the principles on how water is being shared, especially during periods of extended low availability and high demand, i.e., the basic rules being employed while prioritizing water use between agriculture, hydropower, urban and rural supply, environment and recreation during water shortages.

The regulation should also clearly define the water governance arrangements for all levels of government, including the establishment of a national or local water resource council or similar body for providing oversight of strategic management of key water resource issues, assessing the progress of water management improvement implementation and providing implementation support. Often, these agencies are supported by technical and policy-orientated working groups, which also must be prescribed within the regulation.

Water resource management decisions must be evidence-based and underpinned by best available technical information. Generally, this requires a systematic collection of data (e.g., hydro-met, ecological, economic and social) and standardized methods to assess data, and to ensure that a consistent, credible approach is undertaken. A systematic approach is particularly important in the countries that are very large in geographical area or have large populations and complex administrative boundaries, to allow for useful comparisons and tracking of water management improvement progress.

Regular water resource monitoring and reporting provides a means to objectively assess the impact of management interventions across the country or province. Monitoring programs can assess the amount of surface and groundwater available, the types of water users and amount of water they use, the quality of water and the health of river systems. Initial monitoring should establish benchmarks that can be used for reporting and comparative assessments to monitor progress and identify areas for improvement.

Increasing transparency, by making water resource information publicly available, allows for an increased understanding of the on-going changing status of water resources across the country/province and where and why there are changes in water availability. This policy assists individual water users to manage their own risks, particularly during water shortages. For example, an isolated farmer or water user association in the east of Indonesia may access reports (assuming there is access to the internet) to develop a clearer understanding of potential rainfall for the following six months in the region. This information would help farmers make more evidence-based decisions when determining the best type of crops to plant for that season, to efficiently use the water potentially available and receive the highest financial return.

STEP 3: CLARIFY INSTITUTIONAL ROLES AND RESPONSIBILITIES

The water resource sector in both developed and developing countries is complex. It can involve many departments and agencies across all levels of government. In China, for example, it could involve five administrative divisions of government—national, provincial level (33), municipal level (over 300), county-level (over 2,800) and township-level (over 41,600). Therefore, clear definition and transparency of the roles and responsibilities of government institutions are required, including how responsibilities are tied with regulation (i.e. law, national policy and strategies) and aligned between institutions at all levels of government. This process should also assess the limitations of institutions to undertake their assigned responsibilities, to ensure expectations are not over-reached.

Focus should be primarily on separating the main roles of water management between the water service provider (e.g., operating reservoir systems, building wastewater treatments plants, establishing water supply pipeline networks) and the water resource manager (e.g., establishing, issuing and monitoring compliance of water sharing plans and water rights). In particular, the roles and responsibilities for preparing water sharing plans should be clearly defined as the task will likely require input from all departments involved in the water sector. This delineation of responsibilities will help to ensure that information is coordinated and not duplicated between departments, and assist in building trust and stronger relationships between the departments, which will aid the coordination of information, and ultimately, provide for more effective water sharing process.

STEP 4: INCREASE AWARENESS, SUPPORT AND PARTICIPATION

Governments that embrace GWD principles must raise awareness and increase understanding of these principles and their benefits within the government agencies, the private sector and the general public. Raising awareness will help to dispel the belief of water users that they have an unfettered right to water. It will also increase water users' ability to participate in the processes for deciding how water is to be shared, as they will be better informed. This will lead to greater acceptance of why more water is allocated to one water user and less to another, when water availability is less than the demand. An important part of this step is to make transparent the trade-off decisions—the reasons for how the water sharing arrangements came about.

There are many types of communication tools, such as the internet, distributing reports and local community meetings that raise awareness. However, key to effective communication will be ensuring that the interests and current understanding of the targeted audience (e.g., government executives, local farmers) are considered and accommodated. In countries with large population and land size, an extensive, resource intensive campaign can build awareness at the lowest possible administrative levels of the benefits of implementing GWD approach for managing water scarcity. In the first instance, regions where river basins are the most water stressed should be targeted, engaged more intimately and monitored more closely.

*GWD Application through Bank Supported Operations*

The first case of demonstrating the use of GWD approach will be in northern China through the Bank-supported Water Conservation Project II (WCP2) and potentially GEF Hai Basin Integrated Water and Environmental Management Project Phase II (GEF Hai2, in concept stage).

These projects are designed to tackle the priority issues of increasing water scarcity and variability, water pollution and ecological system degradation (e.g., severe groundwater overdraft) (World Bank 2011). Building on the initial achievements of Bank-supported Water Conservation Project (WCP) and GEF Hai Basin Integrated Water and Environmental Management Project (GEF Hai) as well as government's water-saving programs, the following key activities are expected to be piloted and/or scaled up:

INFORMATION/KNOWLEDGE BASE ESTABLISHMENT, MANAGEMENT PLANNING AND IMPLEMENTATION

A comprehensive water resources assessment has been carried out in the Hai Basin; issues and options have been identified; a strategic development and management plan, together with specialized management plans have been formulated; a decision support tool for integrated water and environment management (database, model package and task force in the Hai River Basin Commission) established; Integrated Water and Environment Management Plans (IWEMPs) developed for a pilot tributary and selected municipality and counties; an Evapo-Transpiration (ET)-based water allocation plan developed and disseminated after consultation and regular ET measurement through earth observation satellite for the entire basin is being taken regularly.

The WCP2 and GEF Hai2 projects, aimed at water and environment conservation and agricultural water productivity improvement, will seek to help the government to improve and operationalize the IWEMPs in the project areas, the ET allocation to the respective provinces, municipalities, counties and WUAs (for irrigation and rural uses) and establish ET-based water use right system in a pilot county. At the same time, the basin commission

**Figure 6.1: A comprehensive view of the global observing system for water resources management**

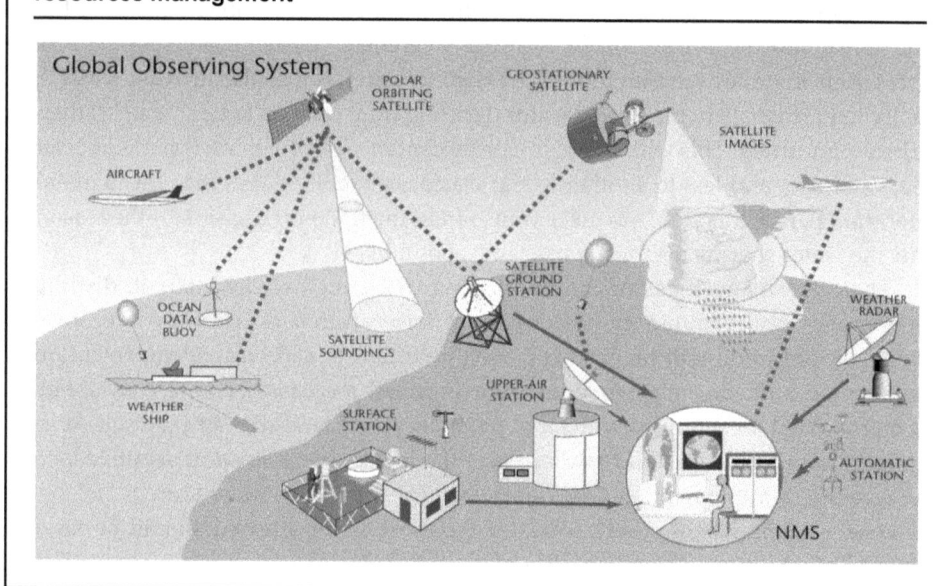

*Source:* Matthew Rodell et al., 2009

and project entities concerned will continue to use remote sensing technology, ground-based hydro-met and groundwater monitoring (see figure 6.1 for an example of global observing system), as well as modeling analysis, to monitor the actual water (consumptive) use, groundwater dynamics and quality of the water bodies, for evaluation of intervention impact and informing decisions on water and environment management.

MULTIPLE-WIN COMPREHENSIVE WATER CONSERVATION

The WCP2 adopts an integrated project design with a comprehensive package of water conservation and productivity improvement measures. It aims to reduce agricultural water consumption and increase agricultural water productivity and farm income. The interventions fall into three categories: engineering/technical, management/institutional and agricultural. These represent modernization of irrigated agriculture geared towards higher productivity with smaller footprint. The technical measures meet the need to upgrade the physical system by making the water supply and distribution more reliable and more efficient. Management measures include enhancing participatory irrigation management through WUA empowerment and capacity building; improving irrigation services by establishing quasi-contractual service relations between irrigation management and farmer water users, and volumetric water charges for irrigation; improving water management effectiveness through better management planning and water consumption monitoring (see figure 6.2 for a ET map for Tongzhou district, Beijing), and targeted water conservation program (of which the Bank projects are a part). The agricultural measures refer to on-farm interventions to save water and increase farm productivity, and include soil moisture preservation measures, water efficient crop varieties, balanced fertilizer applications, etc. The expected results (for WCP2) are: producing *more* (agricul-

**Figure 6.2: ET map in Tongzhou district of Beijing before (left) and after (right) the WCP project**

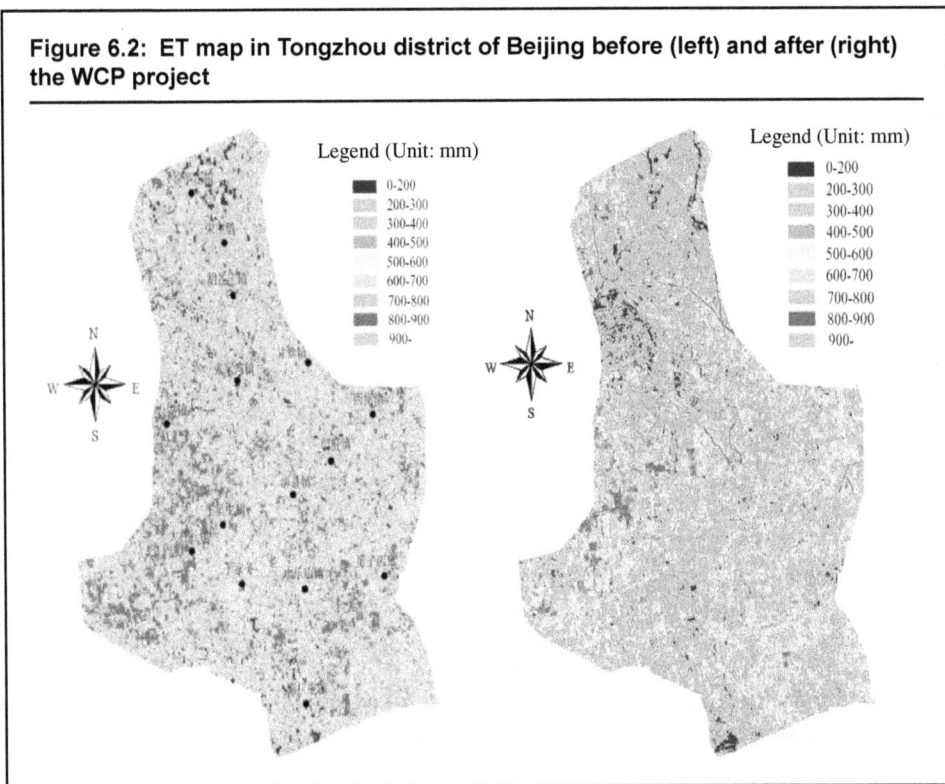

*Source:* World Bank, 2007

tural products of higher value for users) with *less* (water consumed and other production inputs such as fertilizer and energy, and externalities in terms of pollution and overdraft of groundwater, etc.) and improving water and ecological system sustainability.

AWARENESS RAISING AND CAPACITY BUILDING

This involves awareness raising, training and empowerment of management staff and WUAs, and provision of necessary management tools. The WCP2 project will provide support to the 'campaign for building water-conservation society' to raise public awareness and engage water users in water-saving activities. The project management teams at different levels will be provided with training on ET-management, decision-support tools and monitoring technologies. Similarly, WUAs will be trained and empowered to do farm-level water planning and management, operate and maintain the lower canal systems, and participate in groundwater monitoring in groundwater-irrigated areas. The capacity building is expected to help the replication of the good practices established under Bank-supported projects in areas well beyond project borders.

TECHNOLOGICAL AND INSTITUTIONAL INNOVATIONS

Technical innovations, in addition to promoting the use of remote sensing and modeling techniques for ET monitoring and management including the evaluation of water-saving interventions, and cost-effective agricultural water saving technologies, will support applied research on effective surface-groundwater conjunctive use to control

**Figure 6.3: (a) Ground water depletion zone captured by satellite remote sensing and (b) monthly time series of water storage anomalies in NW India**

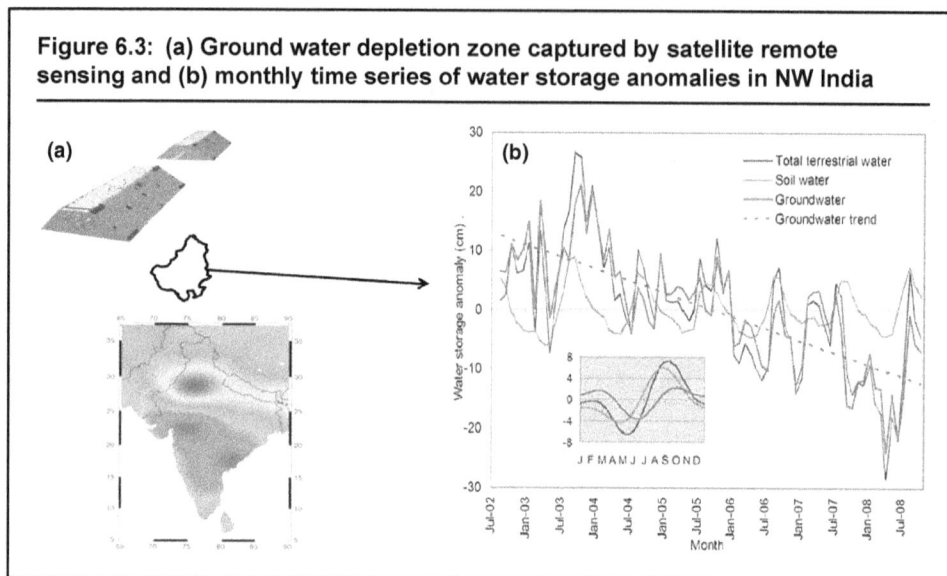

*Source:* Matthew Rodell et al., 2009

soil salinity and on use of brackish shallow groundwater for supplemental irrigation, and best management practices for water-saving and climate-change adaptation in agriculture. Further, the projects will explore using satellite (e.g., GRACE) to predict drought conditions, monitor groundwater changes and surface water quality and agricultural non-point source pollution. This can benefit from the experiences of space agencies such as NASA, in drought and groundwater monitoring undertakings in the Middle-East and South Asia (see figure 6.3 for satellite based estimates of groundwater depletion in NW India).

On the institutional front, the projects will support integrated planning and management at the basin/sub-basin and county level, and participatory irrigation management at the system levels. Institutional mechanisms can be developed for integrated water and environment management for basin and county levels. Demonstration pilots would be undertaken in surface-water and groundwater-irrigated areas respectively towards establishing ET-based water use right system. The ET-based water use right emphasizes consumption and has three elements: water withdrawal, consumption (ET) and return flow. Studies will examine Payment-for-Ecological Services (PES) mechanism for water-saving in areas of groundwater overdraft, and options for trading or transfer of water saved in surface water irrigated areas. These innovations are intended to sustain not only the project activities, but more importantly to contribute to the sustainability of water and related ecological systems in northern China.

# Background to Case Study: Victoria, Australia

## Background to Victoria's Drought Management Regime

In May 2009[1], Victoria's major water storages were at only 12.5 percent of the capacity and Melbourne's water storages had declined to only 26 percent of full capacity. This was the result of the most severe and extended drought ever in South-eastern Australia. The period from 1997 to 2009 saw 13 consecutive years of dry conditions, including the lowest annual inflows to storages ever recorded (2006–07). This unprecedented period of drought, as highlighted in figure A.1, is witnessed by Victoria and the rest of south-eastern Australia to experience conditions that were well outside the boundaries of water management up to that time.

Figure A.2 shows the storage levels for Melbourne's reservoirs in percentage terms. The storages declined from 95 percent at the end of November (the end of the spring

**Figure A.1: Rainfall patterns 1996–2010**

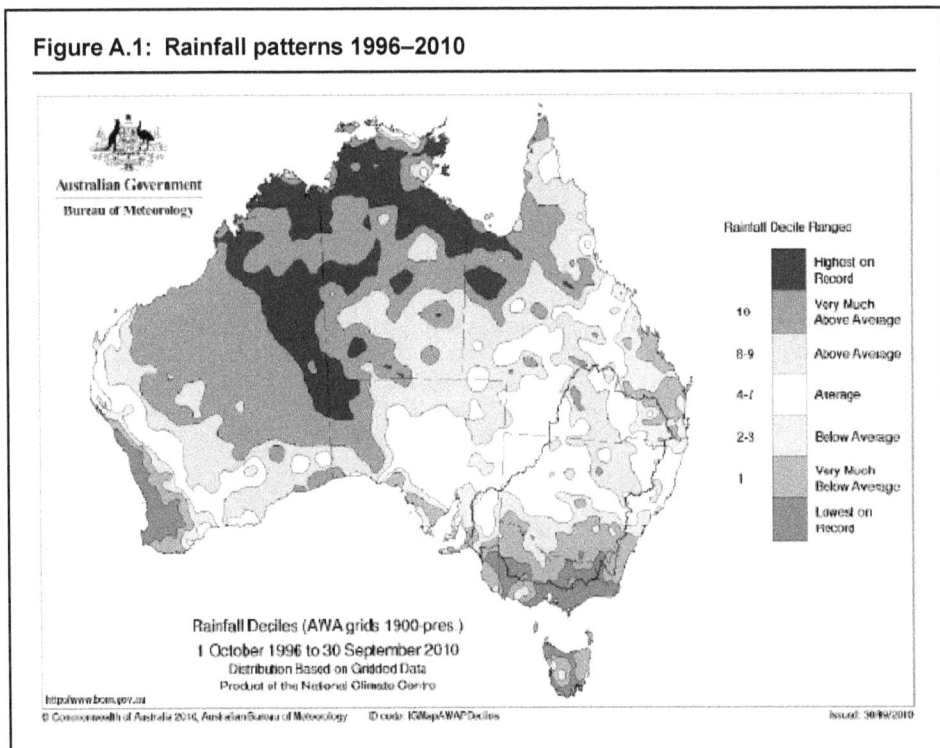

*Source::* Bureau of Meteorology, Australia, 2010

**Figure A.2: Percentage of Melbourne total reservoir storage level, 1993–2010**

November Storage Levels

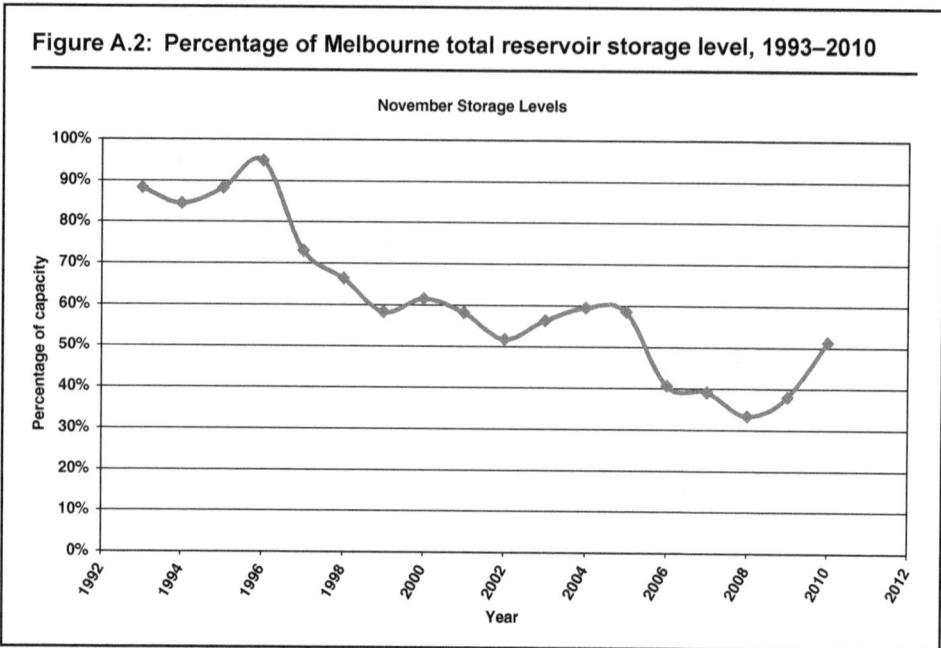

*Source:* Graeme Turner, 2012

harvest period) 1995 to 35 percent at the same time in 2008. There has been a small recovery of storage levels over 2009 and a more significant increase through 2010 as a result of well above average rainfall in that year. As highlighted in figure A.3, Australia has one of the most variable climates in the World with runoff variability[2] almost twice that of all the other continents and regions except Southern Africa[3]. The south eastern Australian extended drought is the result of this natural variability and also climate change[4].

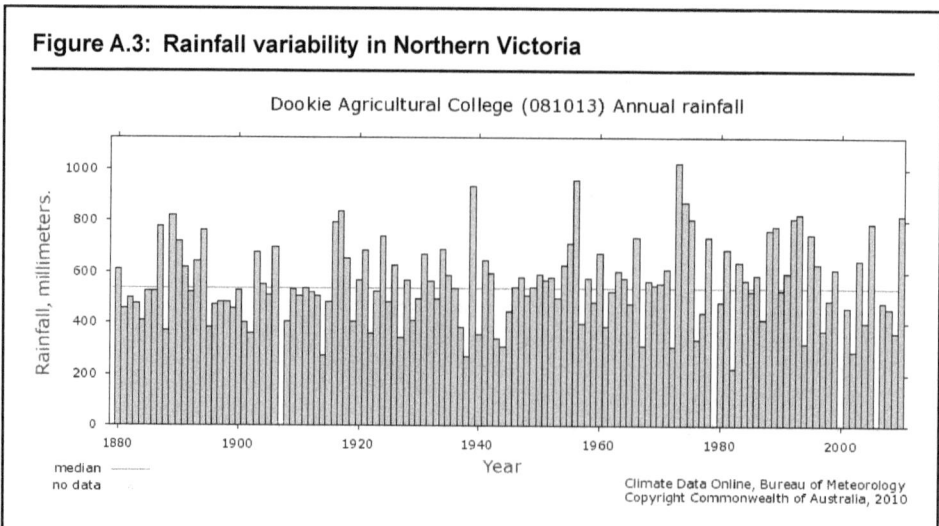

**Figure A.3: Rainfall variability in Northern Victoria**

Dookie Agricultural College (081013) Annual rainfall

median
no data

Climate Data Online, Bureau of Meteorology
Copyright Commonwealth of Australia, 2010

*Source:* Bureau of Meteorology, Australia, 2010

Dartmouth reservoir, the largest reservoir in Victoria and Thomson serving Melbourne, had only, respectively 57 percent and 37 percent of the capacity in January 2011. These remaining storages in the reservoir serve as the main buffer storages against extended drought. The total water in storage for Melbourne in January 2011 was just above 50 percent of full capacity. Although 2010 was a good year for rainfall and storage inflows, a full recovery from the extended drought is still not assured.

Victoria's storage systems have played a critical role in the management of drought to date. They have given the government time to respond to the uncertain future. This response has been multi-faceted, involving major investment in irrigation efficiency, conservation, recycling, pipelines to provide alternative supplies and a large desalination plant.

The Victorian water management story is more than a question of adequate infrastructure provision. Water management in Victoria is included progressive legislature, institutional reform and development and infrastructure investment over more than 130 years. Improvement and refinement has been incremental and progressive with each change building on the past structures.

The current major challenges are to meet the needs of continuing population growth and related development at the same time as increasing environmental water provision within a background of uncertainty relating to the future impacts of Climate Change. However, Victoria is well placed to meet this challenge given the legal, institutional and infrastructure structures in place.

The following sections provide an insight to Victoria's water management capacity, in particular the institutional framework, and legal structures and infrastructure flexibility that have enabled the State to successfully manage the recent challenges and will enable future challenges to be met.

## The Legal Water Entitlement Framework

Up until 1886 in Victoria, common law riparian access rights were in effect. In 1886, Alfred Deakin (a future Australian Prime Minister) introduced legislation (*The Irrigation Act 1886*) into the Victorian Parliament which vested all rights to water with the government (the Crown). This handing of primary right to the Crown has been the cornerstone of Victorian water law reform ever since and remains so with the current version of the Victorian Water Act (*The Water Act 1989*). The current hierarchy of water rights is summarized in figure A.4.

The Victorian legislative framework is a three tier rights system. as mentioned, the primary right is with the Victorian Government which grants secondary rights with conditions to urban and rural water authorities who, in turn, are responsible for providing water to individuals as tertiary rights with conditions.

This strict hierarchy of rights and the attached conditions applied to the second and third tier rights have been one of the keys to successful management of water shortage over this period of the current drought, as it has through many previous droughts. The key features of this entitlement system are:

- Primacy of Government rights which is particularly important in terms of drought management as it allows, under the Water act, for the second- and third-tier rights to be temporarily "qualified" under extreme dry conditions;
- Secure entitlements—legal rights that are certain and protected;

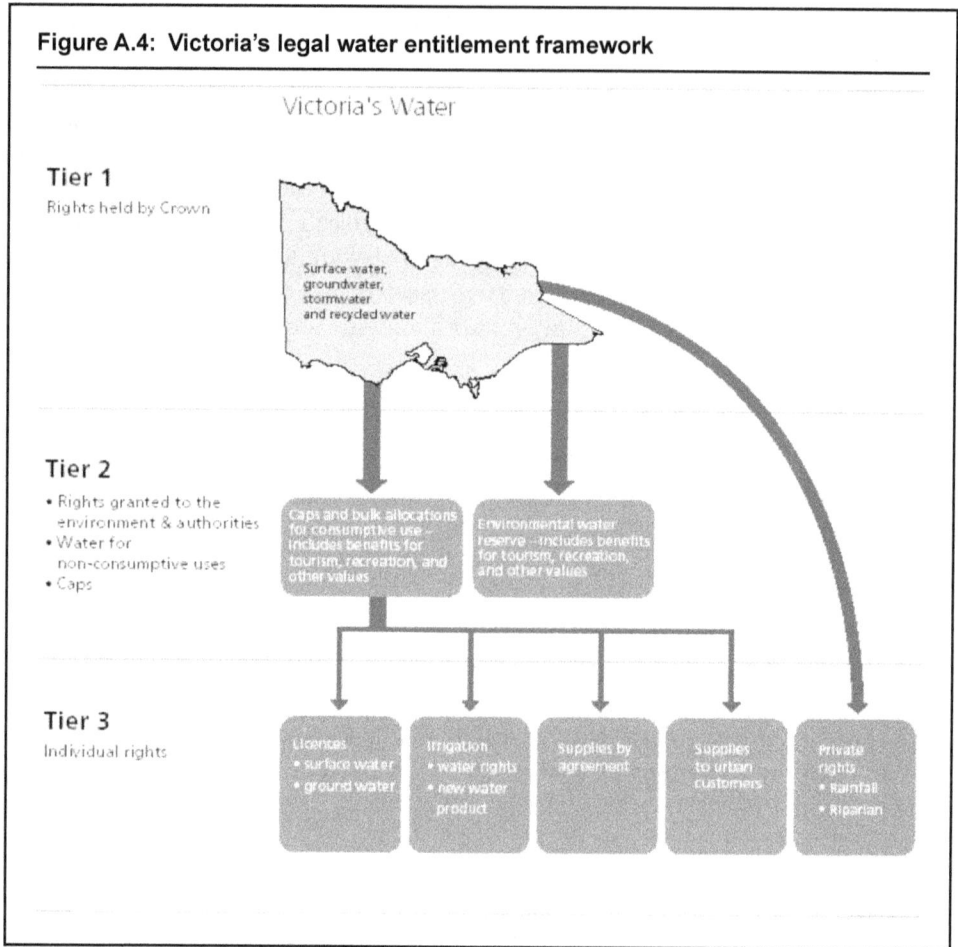

Figure A.4:  Victoria's legal water entitlement framework

*Source:* National Water Commission, 2011c

- Limits on water entitlements—i.e., specified volumes, extraction rates and locations, diversion rules, sharing arrangements;
- Annual processes to allocate water to entitlements;
- Clear responsibilities between the Government and the various entitlement holders;
- Clear consultative processes before entitlements are changed; and
- Ability of water entitlement holders to buy and sell entitlements on a water market to allow entitlement holders to adjust to varying circumstances without interference by the government.

The Tier 2 rights to water (bulk and environmental entitlements) for most systems establish the rules for managing the water resources, specifying:

- The total amount of water that can be harvested by the system;
- The minimum flow requirements of the regulated rivers downstream of the reservoirs;
- The reserve and allocation rules to be implemented by the storage manager; and

**Figure A.5:  System bulk entitlement characteristics**

Conditions on entitlements
• maximum release from storage
• maximum extraction from weir
• minimum passing flow(s)
• storage sharing between A and B

Obligations
• metering
• reporting
• cost sharing
• environmental impact of works

Inflows

Evaporation

Storage

River losses

Extraction by Tier 2
Entitlement holder A

Diversion Weir

Extraction by Tier 2
Entitlement holder B

Delivery to
Tier 3 water share
& other rights to water

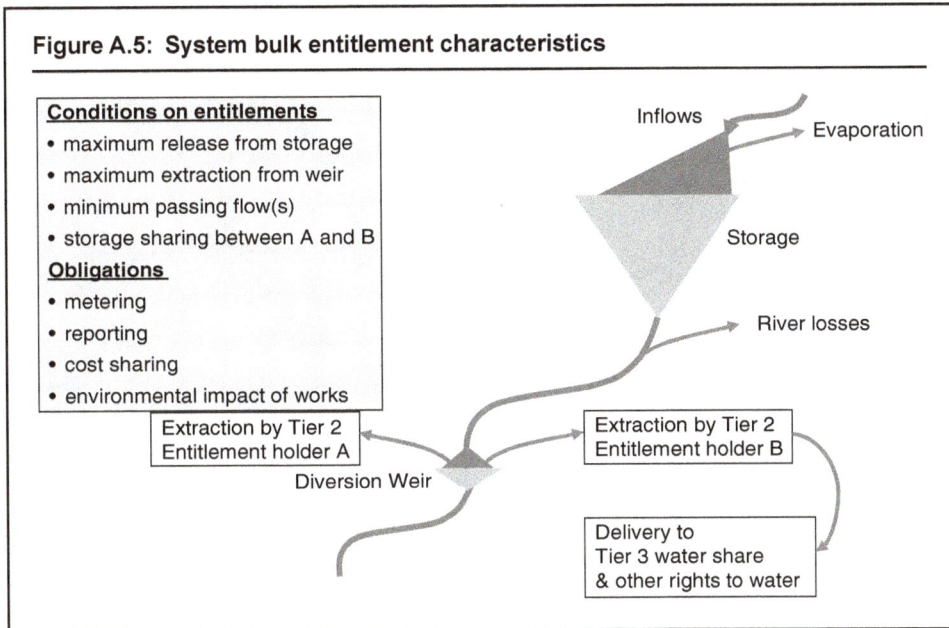

*Source:*  Graeme Turner, 2012

- The primary entitlements or commitments (e.g., water shares, delivery bulk entitlements and environmental entitlements) to be supplied from the water in the system.

The key attributes of a typical system bulk entitlement are presented in Figure A.5.

## The Institutional Framework

The institutional framework, prescribed in the Victorian Water act, has four major areas of operation:

- Government undertakes policy and planning development, establishes financial priorities and monitors a broad range of performance;
- Water authorities manage the harvesting, treatment and distribution of water to the communities;
- Customer committees, government advisory groups, appointment of community representative boards and vocal and politically aware communities are all features of a diverse system of communication and exchange; and
- Government appointed commissions and authorities provide strong and effective regulation and monitoring of financial, public health and environmental impacts, ensuring water authorities are responsible for on-going sustainable infrastructure, regulation of performance and impact on the community and environment.

All water authorities generate revenue by charging for water deliveries and associated services. Urban water authorities are predominantly self funding, and rural water authorities self fund on-going operation but periodically receive considerable government support for infrastructure modernization.

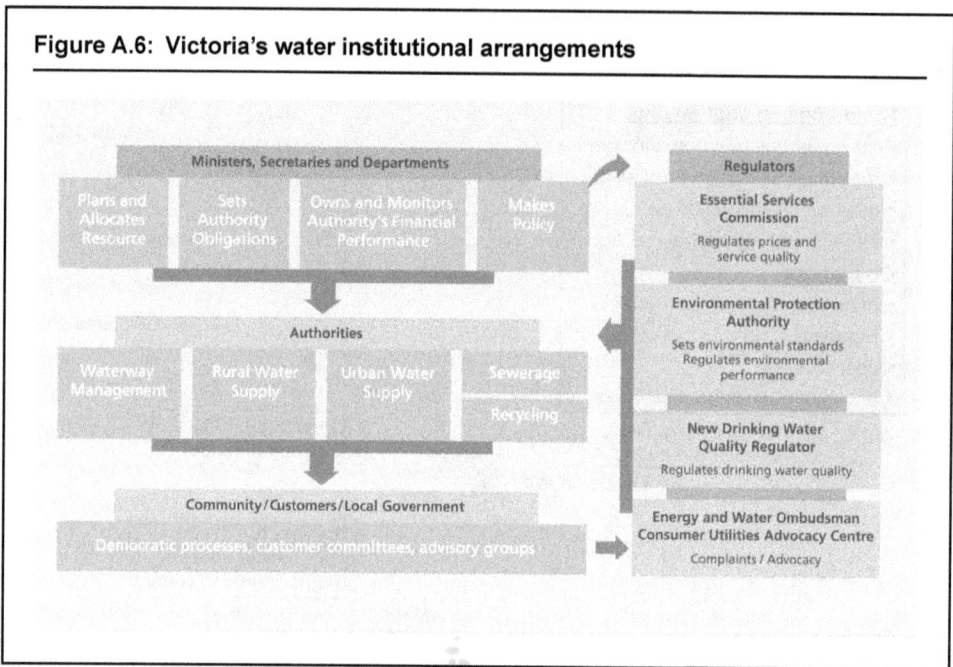

Figure A.6: Victoria's water institutional arrangements

*Source:* National Water Commission, 2011

The institutional framework is summarized in figure A.6.

A key aspect of the institutional structure of the Victorian water industry is that the water authorities are state owned and accountable and they are responsive to their customers who contribute significantly to their operation and who have a strong interest in their effective management. This accountability to both the government owner and the communities they serve, while sometimes difficult to manage, generally results in better outcomes to problems, issues and external challenges such as drought.

## Change and Response to Change, 1980–2010

The last 30 years have been a period of major change in terms of increased competition for water, economy and climate. The Victorian water industry has responded to these changes by amending the Water Act, enhancing institutional reform, providing infrastructure and operational improvements. These changes and the responses to them are highlighted below:

■ **Water industry viability.** Prior to 1980, the Victorian water industry consisted of two major "public works" departments and more than 400 small to large urban and rural water trusts often attached to municipal councils. This institutional structure presented numerous problems, particularly relating to financial viability, efficiency and effectiveness of service delivery and responsiveness. The structure was somewhat antiquated: it contained significant and nontransparent subsidy and there was little motivation for improvement. Commencing around 1980 and continuing for more than 15 years, the Victorian government undertook a major restructuring of the water industry. The water industry was transformed into one urban water wholesale authority, three suburban and 15 regional urban water authorities and four regional irrigation authorities all with the single focus of water management. The restructuring has enabled water authorities to become financially viable and more fully accountable, effective and efficient;

- **Environmental degradation in river systems.** There has been growing concern about the environmental condition of all river systems has been growing for many years. Victoria has responded to this, initially by recognizing the environment as a legitimate user of water in the 1989 Water act, by developing major policy including the 2002 Victorian River Health Strategy, the 2004 *Government White Paper, Securing Our Water Future Together (Our Water Our Future)* and monitoring and reporting on river health[5] to reference changes. Victoria is investing in stream rehabilitation to reverse past degradation. The investment, as well as reducing consumption diversions and increasing environmental flows, includes catchment and riparian habitat restoration and increased provision of environmental flows;

- **Murray-Darling river system: over-allocation and environmental condition.** By the early 1990's consumption in the Murray-Darling River system had, on average, exceeded 80 percent of what had naturally flowed to the sea. The Council of Australian Governments (COAG) met in 1992 to respond to a need for the Federal and State Governments to act cooperatively in dealing with social, economic and environmental matters across state boundaries and national in scope and solution. Water allocation was one such issue. The initial action was setting of a "Cap" on use to 1993–94 levels of development by agreement of the Murray-darling Basin Ministerial Council. This has been followed progressively by major initiatives such as the national Water initiative, Living Murray, Snowy intergovernmental agreements and the Murray-darling Basin plan, all aimed at winding back irrigation diversions and recovering water for the environment, principally through reduction in irrigation delivery losses;

- **The 1997–2009 Drought.** This crisis has motivated and accelerated a range of responses ranging from major policy initiatives (*Our Water Our Future*, etc.), major infrastructure provision and improved system management. In rural areas considerable support and investment improved on-farm irrigation efficiency and in urban areas considerable attention and investment has been made to reduce water consumption. In both the rural and urban areas, success has been achieved in consumption reduction; and

- **Increasing awareness of climate change impact.** This awareness has resulted in greater commitment to planning, investing in irrigation modernization and Federal-State government co-operation in dealing with water resource allocation. The greater awareness of the long-term implications of climate change highlighted through the experience of the unprecedented recent drought has added to the urgency to address the water resource sharing issues that became evident during the recent drought.

The timing and interaction between the changes are demonstrated diagrammatically in figure A.7, which highlights several key aspects of this period of change, namely:

- The judicious timing of the water industry restructuring at the beginning of this period of change prepared Victoria and its water industry for the challenges ahead in dealing with the other changes;

Figure A.7:  Major influences on the Victoria's water industry, 1980–2010

1980                                                                    2010

Overallocation

Water
Industry
Restructuring

Environmental degradation

Drought

Climate change

1980                                                                    2010

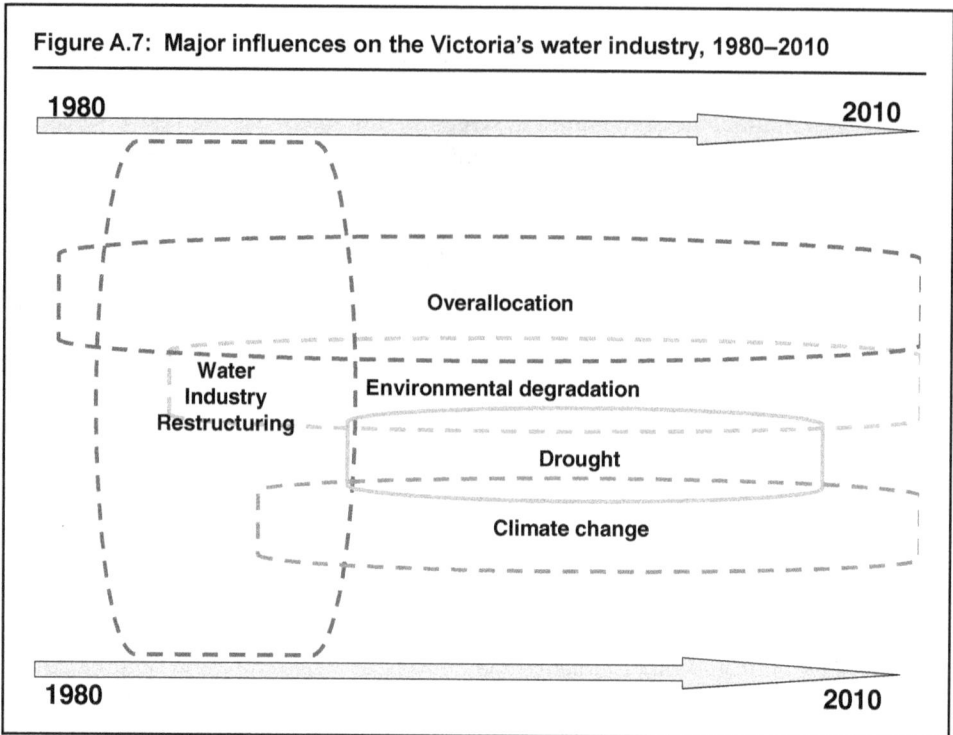

*Source:* Graeme Turner, 2012

- The beginning and end of most of the changes, with the possible exception of drought are not precise or easily quantified; and
- There is a high degree of interaction between the changes. Over-allocation and drought resulted in environmental degradation, and drought and climate change have had an indeterminate yet certain interface. This demonstrates the high level of interaction between the changes. Also, the timing of industry restructuring was critical in preparing Victoria and its water industry for the challenges ahead.

## The Elements of Successful Water Resource Management

*Providing Certainty and Flexibility*

The capability of Victoria to deal with severe drought is based on providing both certainty and flexibility. (See figure A.8)

The core of this capability is secure entitlements to water. Secure entitlements provide certainty and clarity regarding responsibility for actions which are supported by the following:

- Provision of infrastructure to enable water to be delivered where and when required, particularly during drought periods;
- Limits to shorter term and yearly use under entitlements;
- Annual allocations based on entitlements and entitlement sharing principles as defined in the Water Act and Bulk entitlements; and
- Trade and carryover for Tier 2 and Tier 3 entitlement holders allow individuals to adjust to emerging drought in a manner suited their needs.

**Figure A.8: The Victoria's way: water management with certainty and flexibility**

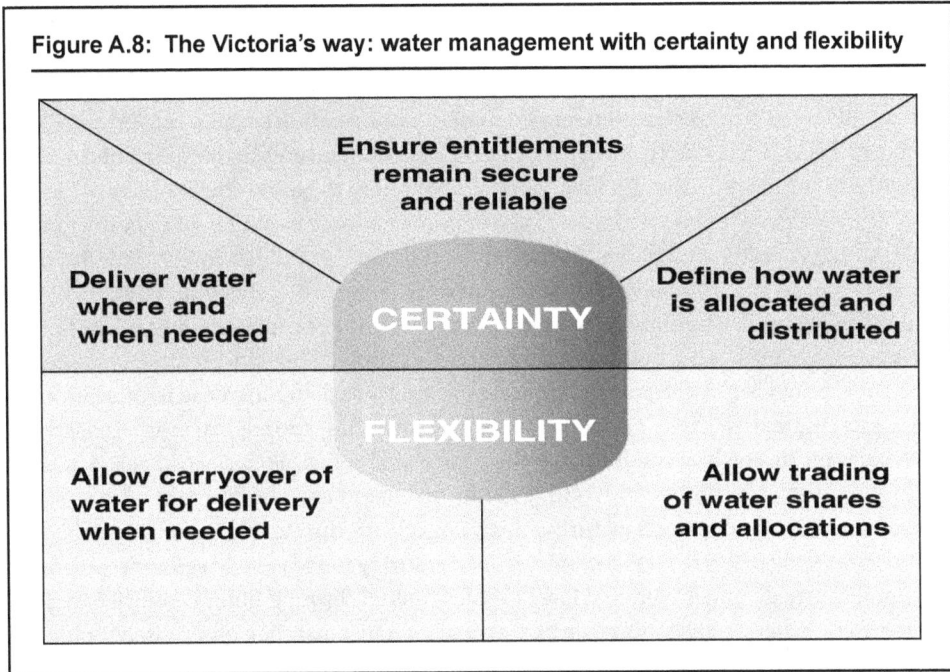

Ensure entitlements
remain secure
and reliable

Deliver water
where and
when needed

CERTAINTY

Define how water
is allocated and
distributed

FLEXIBILITY

Allow carryover of
water for delivery
when needed

Allow trading
of water shares
and allocations

*Source:* Department of Sustainability and Environment, 2009

The following paragraphs describe particular aspects of drought management in Victoria in greater detail both from a general perspective and in terms of the experience during recent extreme drought.

### Annual Allocations for Irrigation in Major Irrigation Systems

Irrigation consumes approximately 70 percent of all water used in Victoria. The major irrigation systems are in northern Victoria and are supplied by the Goulburn and Murray River major reservoirs. The annual allocation system for the northern irrigation areas is critical to orderly distribution of water and continuity of supply over extended dry periods. at the start of the water year[6] and then periodically over the irrigation season, the Tier 2 entitlement holder (i.e. Goulburn-Murray Water for Northern Victorian irrigation areas) makes a percentage allocation to each Tier 3 entitlement (i.e. an individual irrigator) based on the water available in the system.

In determining an allocation, the Tier 2 entitlement holder has regard to the operating rules and obligations in the bulk entitlements. Firstly, water in storage plus conservatively assumed future inflows over the irrigation period are defined as the 'available water.' System delivery losses, environmental passing flows and urban entitlement volumes are then deducted from the available water and the remainder is then available for allocation to irrigation entitlement holders. Initial losses such as channel filling and variable losses such as leakage, uncontrolled releases, evaporation and under recording meters are considered. Delivery losses of up to 35 percent of water diverted were historically common, but have been reduced through modernization.

On the Goulburn system, for example, over 400 GL of additional water is required before a commitment can be made on deliveries to Tier 3 (irrigators) entitlement holders.

Any Tier 3 allocation is then distributed in proportion to the entitlement volume held by individual entitlement holders.

Because inflows generally improve from what has been assumed initially, allocations will increase at least until the mid-point of the irrigation season. In wet years when storages are full or close to full, it is possible to commence with 100 percent allocation but, in dry years with storages low, zero is more likely to be the starting allocation.

The past decade has demonstrated a risk in the forecasting of inflows for the purpose of determining allocations. The 2006–07 inflows were much lower than the previously recorded minimums. Water allocations for some water systems outside Victoria had to be reduced when the predicted inflows did not occur. Reducing allocation can have severe effects on farm planning and urban supply. Thus, in Victoria, considerable caution is practiced in determining initial allocations and any increase in allocations.

Since the early 2000s, Goulburn-Murray Water has adopted a more conservative approach for forecasting inflows over the year ahead when no carryover reserve for the following year is available. Now, forecast inflows are based on the rate of recession of the current flows and assume no further high flow events during that season. The allocation is increased only if more water becomes available during the season. In some circumstances, where it can be demonstrated that losses are less (either through tighter control of delivery or reduced demand), allocations can be increased above what they otherwise would be.

Following construction of major storages after the severe drought of the 1940s, and until 2002, there had always been enough Goulburn River flow each year to meet the system operating requirement and provide more than 100 percent allocation (end of season) to the holders of high-reliability entitlements.

The prolonged dry conditions between 1997 and 2009 resulted in allocations reduced to no greater than 100 percent of full entitlement in the Goulburn system. In 2002–03, the Goulburn system final allocation was 57 percent, the first time allocations were less than 100 percent in over 50 years. For the four years from 2006–07 to 2009–10, the Goulburn system allocations remained well below 100 percent. In 2006–07, final allocations for the Goulburn system were a record low of 29 percent.

The drought continued to diminish inflows until 2007–08, when there was insufficient water in the Goulburn system at the start of August (when the channel system is normally charged with water ready for the irrigation season to start on August 15) to meet system operating water needs. For the first time in recent history, the starting seasonal allocation was zero.

## 2007 Special Management Provisions

By 2007 water availability had deteriorated to levels requiring extreme drought management measures. Up to then, the normal management tools available under entitlements and allocation rules provided confidence in continued availability of adequate water. The response to these extreme conditions was layered and ranged from high level policy adjustment to very practical operational measures. In broad terms the response was as follows:

- Establishing a Dry Inflow Contingency Planning Group to guide the development of measures to reduce the impact of drought. This group played a key role in developing specific drought management measures and in communicating these to the broader affected communities;

- Affirmation of existing policy objectives and management arrangements that to clarify priorities for water use, most efficient delivery of water, continuity of management and as much certainty as possible to users;
- Major review of distribution systems, in particular irrigation systems to minimize water losses. The review included closing down non-essential parts of the distribution systems, tighter delivery operation to minimize outfalls and unauthorized use, reducing the length of irrigation season and pumping "dead" storage volumes;
- Review and adjustment of management rules such as restrictions policies to reflect the extreme nature of the circumstances. Community response to tighter restrictions was generally highly supportive, particularly when the need was adequately communicated;
- Establishing priorities of use: the Water act contains priority of use principles, the basis of more detailed guidelines for progressive right to water ranging from critical human needs through stock use, to industrial use, critical environmental needs and fire fighting;
- Allowing some adjustment to certain policies relating to carryover of allocations and rules on trade to provide individuals with the capacity to minimize the impact in terms of their particular circumstances; and
- Permitting reduction of environmental flow requirements but with compensation provided via innovative approaches to minimize resulting impacts.

The Water act provides the Minister for Water with the power to qualify rights to bring into effect some of the above measures where necessary. Administrative principles and processes underpin these powers and ensure each qualification is consistent and the need properly demonstrated. Many of these adjustments to policy and management are now being built into normal (non-extreme drought) management.

## Water Markets and Trade

Under the Victorian Water Act, trade in entitlements is permitted on a permanent or temporary basis. Since the mid 1990's major water users in northern Victoria have increasingly used the water market as part of their normal management program. The annual growth of trade is shown in figure A.9.

As shown in figure A.9, the volume of trade has increased as water has become scarcer beyond 2002–03. Price trends have also reflected the scarcity of water. In 2009–10, a year with higher allocations on the Goulburn and Murray systems, the market price for water allocation dropped significantly compared to earlier years of severe drought.

The use of trading as a management tool depends significantly on the type of farming enterprise and other personal and financial circumstances. The greater the diversity of uses of water and the timing of demands for water, the greater the likelihood of a more active market.

In Victoria (and throughout the Southern Murray-Darling Basin), the agricultural uses can be classified into three broad categories, annual cropping, dairy farming and horticulture. Annual cropping (cereals and fodder crops) is the most flexible enterprise. These farmers may sell their water allocation when prices are high and return to dry land cropping or grazing. Dairy farmers may also sell their allocations and purchase fodder or grain instead. However, horticulturalists must generally use their water allocation

Figure A.9:  Growth in annually permanent and temporary trading volumes

Volume of permanent and temporary trade (1992~2006)

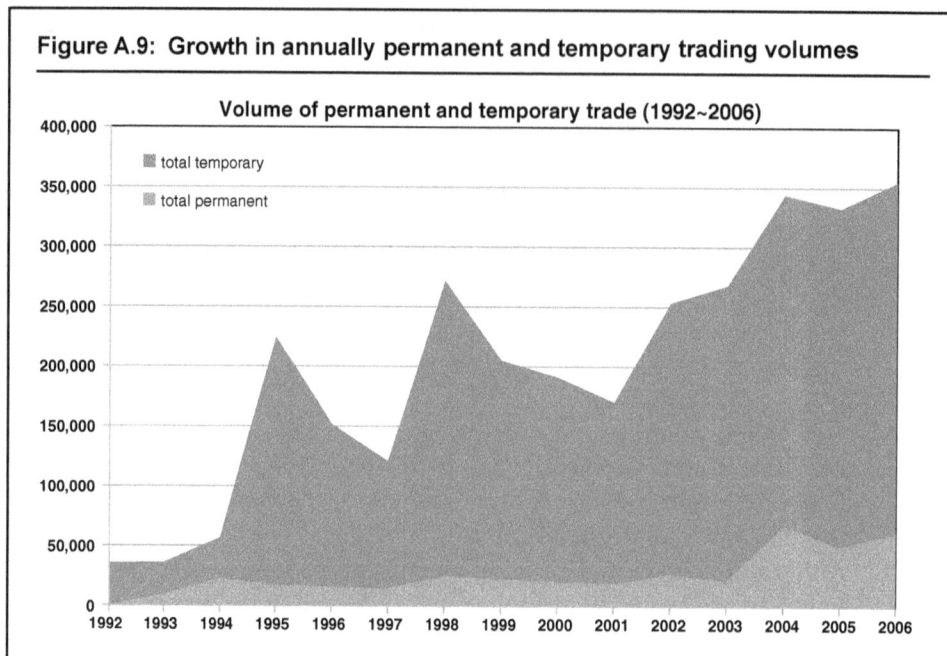

*Source:* National Water Commission, 2010

and may also purchase more allocation during years of drought. Differences in the patterns of use during the irrigation season enhance trading conditions. During the irrigation season, horticulturalists are likely to purchase allocations early and dairy farmers and annual cropping farmers later.

At the height of the drought in 2006–07, water entitlements were unbundled (detached) from land in Northern Victoria. Unbundling facilitated trade and was a timely intervention, making it easier for people to use the water market at that critical time. Drought also forced increased scrutiny and rigor of trading rules and processes responding to customer queries and challenges.

Higher allocations in New South Wales in recent years have increased the volume of water available on the market, providing northern Victorian irrigators, businesses and environmental managers with the option to purchase water from other supply systems such as the Murrumbidgee.

Over the last few years there has been net trade of water shares out of some areas and into other areas, a result of movement either from marginal land to more productive areas or from one form of agriculture to another. The trade movements highlight the importance of the trade in facilitating adjustment by individuals to meet their particular circumstances.

## Carryover and Carryover Changes

Carryover permits entitlement holders to retain a proportion of their water allocations from one year in storage and to use the water in the following year. Carryover was introduced in the Northern Victoria irrigation systems in 2006–07 as a short-term drought contingency measure, allowing irrigators to mitigate the consequences of low starting seasonal allocations. It has since been made a permanent measure, allowed individuals to manage their own risks of supplies in the future, recognizing that entitlement holders are best placed to judge and manage their own needs. Carryover facility encourages efficient use of water and removes the past "use-it-or-lose-it" approach to unused allocation. Previously unused water was included in the 'allocation pool' for the following season. Adoption of the carryover policy had the potential to lower allocations in the following year effectively reducing the availability of water to high water users in normal years. The community considered that the benefits associated with encouraging increased use efficiency outweigh the cost to high water users.

The carryover rules have been refined and now allow entitlement holders to carryover an unlimited volume, provided that airspace in the storages is available. For the new rules, the carried over water is lost if there is a spill of water from that storage, the new rule provides greater flexibility to self manage risks.

Carryover has been increasingly used as the drought and low allocations continued. For example, approximately 130 GL was carried over on the Goulburn and Murray systems at the end of the 2006–07 season compared with approximately 270 GL at the end of the 2008–09 season. Carryover allows irrigators to have water available at crucial times for their businesses regardless of the allocations at that time. For example, sufficient water availability is important early in the season for bud set or fruit set periods for horticulturalists and dairy and cropping farmers require water during spring. Carryover is particularly important for all irrigators during low allocation years because it allows access to water at the beginning of the season when allocations are low or zero.

Carryover allows environmental water managers greater flexibility in managing key environmental assets and ensuring survival of aquatic plants and animals during drought years. When allocations are very low, water carried over from previous years provides a minimum supply, provides base flows in river systems and top-up drought refuges. In wet years, water carried over floods important wetlands, such as Barmah Forest and Gunbower Forest.

Urban water authorities use carryover to help manage through dry years and avoid severe water restrictions, enabling urban "critical human needs" to be met during severe water shortages. Hence, carryover is one mechanism water authorities may use to meet these needs, while reduces the need for government intervention to qualifying rights.

Improved carryover arrangements are expanding the time reach of the market. No longer does the end of an irrigation season mean total uncertainty about water availability. While new allocations will be totally dependent on storage levels and inflows, individuals can use the market during one season to set themselves up for future seasons.

## Reserve Rule and Reserve Rule Changes

Bulk entitlements contain rules to calculate resource availability and allocate it or keep it in reserve for the following year. These "system reserve policies" manage year-to-year variability and determine the volume and reliability of water supplied by the entitlement. Prior to the drought, reserve allocations were only provided after reaching of 100 percent allocation. In this way the reserve rule did not affect on entitlement values. However, the drought has resulted in modifying this rule. Modeling for the northern Region Sustainable Water Strategy[7] shown that without a change to this rule the likelihood of zero or very low allocations increase significantly under Climate Change projections. A change of the rule provided greater certainty that there would be sufficient water in storage for the irrigation system to operate and that a zero allocation is avoided. This is important in ensuring an operational water market to allow the reallocation of water in severe droughts.

The reserve rule has been revised (involving amendment of the Gouburn system bulk entitlement) and now requires the rebuilding of reserve to begin at the start of the irrigation season and to run parallel with allocations. This new rule has been modeled and it has been shown that the impact is to reduce years of 100 percent allocation but with the benefit of avoiding any years of zero allocation and relatively small (1 percent) overall reduction in allocations.

## Meeting the Future Challenges

*Overview*

Recognizing that future climate conditions are uncertain, Victoria has taken a number of steps to ensure that secure water supply is available into the future, including:

- **Planning reviews.** The Victorian Water act prescribes regular review of the long term water resource circumstances and regional sustainable water strategies. In addition, as set out in figure A.10, there are shorter term reviews of water supply/demand and river health. As already discussed, drought response planning and water allocation are undertaken annually. Both long to short term review process has been established as prescribed by the Water act;
- **Strategic planning.** This commenced with the 2004 major Victorian Government White paper, *Our Water Our Future*[8] with follow up policy development to identify all necessary elements of Victoria's response to the extreme drought

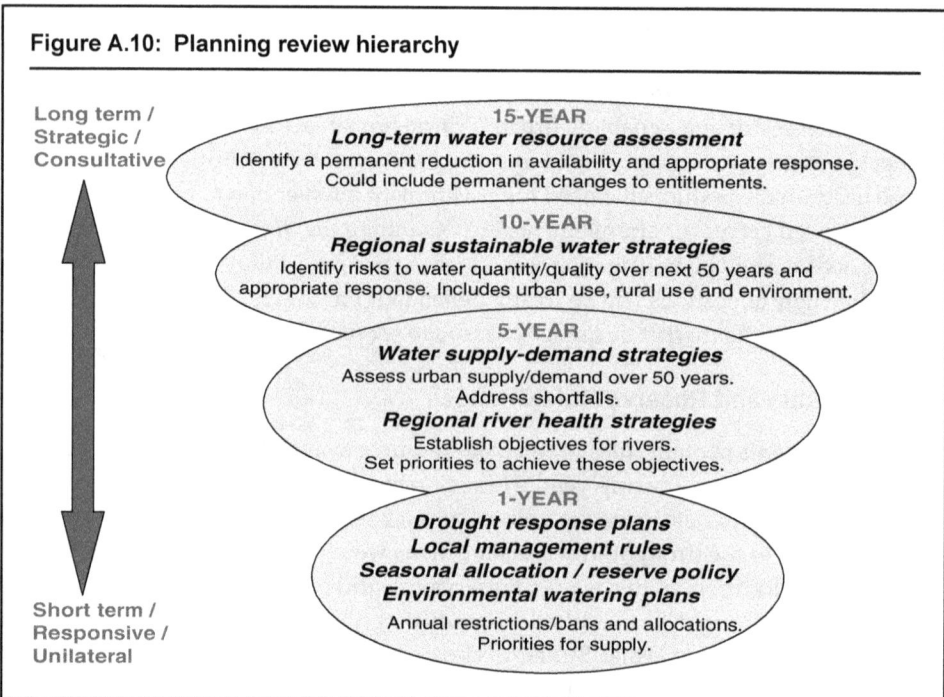

**Figure A.10: Planning review hierarchy**

Long term / Strategic / Consultative

**15-YEAR**
*Long-term water resource assessment*
Identify a permanent reduction in availability and appropriate response. Could include permanent changes to entitlements.

**10-YEAR**
*Regional sustainable water strategies*
Identify risks to water quantity/quality over next 50 years and appropriate response. Includes urban use, rural use and environment.

**5-YEAR**
*Water supply-demand strategies*
Assess urban supply/demand over 50 years. Address shortfalls.
*Regional river health strategies*
Establish objectives for rivers. Set priorities to achieve these objectives.

**1-YEAR**
*Drought response plans*
*Local management rules*
*Seasonal allocation / reserve policy*
*Environmental watering plans*
Annual restrictions/bans and allocations. Priorities for supply.

Short term / Responsive / Unilateral

*Source:* National Water Commission, 2011

conditions. The Water act prescribed regional Sustainable Water Strategies (SWS) to deal with detailed future requirements;

▪ **Major infrastructure augmentation.** Arising from the strategic planning, major supply infrastructure commenced. This infrastructure will help ensure long term security of supply to major urban centers. This infrastructure augmentation and purpose are described later;

▪ **Review of legal and institutional structures.** This on-going process ensures these structures are capable of meeting future challenges. These changes are often recommended as a result of the strategic planning or the statutory required 15 year reviews of bulk and environmental entitlements;

▪ **Monitoring.** Monitoring the effectiveness of recently introduced water management policies (e.g., reserve and carryover) over a number of years to allow, if necessary, adjustment to ensure the policy rules are optimized;

▪ **Water supply demand strategies.** Within the framework of the regional sustainable water strategies, detailed authority by authority water supply-demand planning is being undertaken and is reviewed in 5 yearly increments to match expected changing conditions; and

▪ **Feedback from drought management.** The experience and knowledge gained from short-term planning associated with drought management informs the long term planning process. Drought management has provided invaluable understanding of the capacity of city dwellers and irrigators to respond to periods of reduced supply. The applicability of these responses to the longer term conditions is being better understood through this process.

The process of adjustment through planning is showing in schematic form in figure A.11. Key features of this planning process are the level of integration and the importance of certain tools of the management framework (consultation, carryover and trade) to both short and long term planning.

**Figure A.11: Short- and long-term planning**

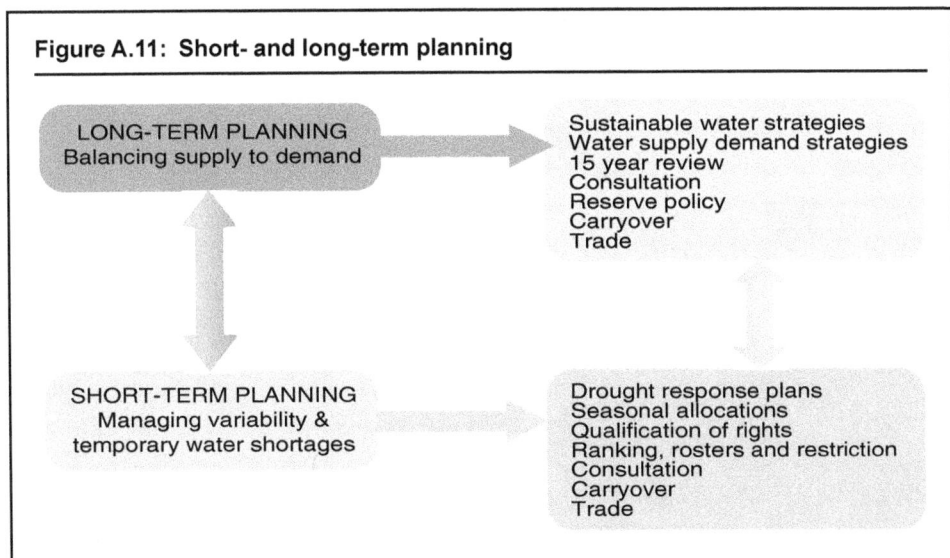

LONG-TERM PLANNING
Balancing supply to demand

Sustainable water strategies
Water supply demand strategies
15 year review
Consultation
Reserve policy
Carryover
Trade

SHORT-TERM PLANNING
Managing variability &
temporary water shortages

Drought response plans
Seasonal allocations
Qualification of rights
Ranking, rosters and restriction
Consultation
Carryover
Trade

*Source:* Victorian Government, 2007

## Our Water Our Future and Strategic Infrastructure

A major infrastructure program was developed based on *Our Water Our Future*, and aimed at securing water supply into the future. The policy report[9] detailing the infrastructure provision, completed in mid June 2007, at a time when the drought was in its tenth year and showed no sign of ending, along with major urban storages approaching only 25 percent of capacity. In addition, there was concern that the observed extended dry climate period was, at least in part, due to climate change.

The major elements of this new infrastructure provision, shown in figure a.12, are:

- A major desalination plant for Melbourne capable of producing up to 200,000 ML of potable water from sea water;
- Modernization of the Goulburn-Murray irrigation district to reduce irrigation losses and redirect the savings to provide extra water for farmers, the environment and urban supply. The additional supply from this source is expected to total more than 500,000 ML;
- Expansion of a system of water supply pipelines which to be called the Victorian Water Grid. The Water Grid provides efficient delivery of water to scattered communities and major regional cities from a diversity of secure supply sources;
- Upgrading a major sewage treatment plant to provide high quality treated water for industrial, commercial and agricultural uses; and
- Expansion of water conservation programs for homes and industry.

**Figure A.12: Victoria's water infrastructure provision against drought**

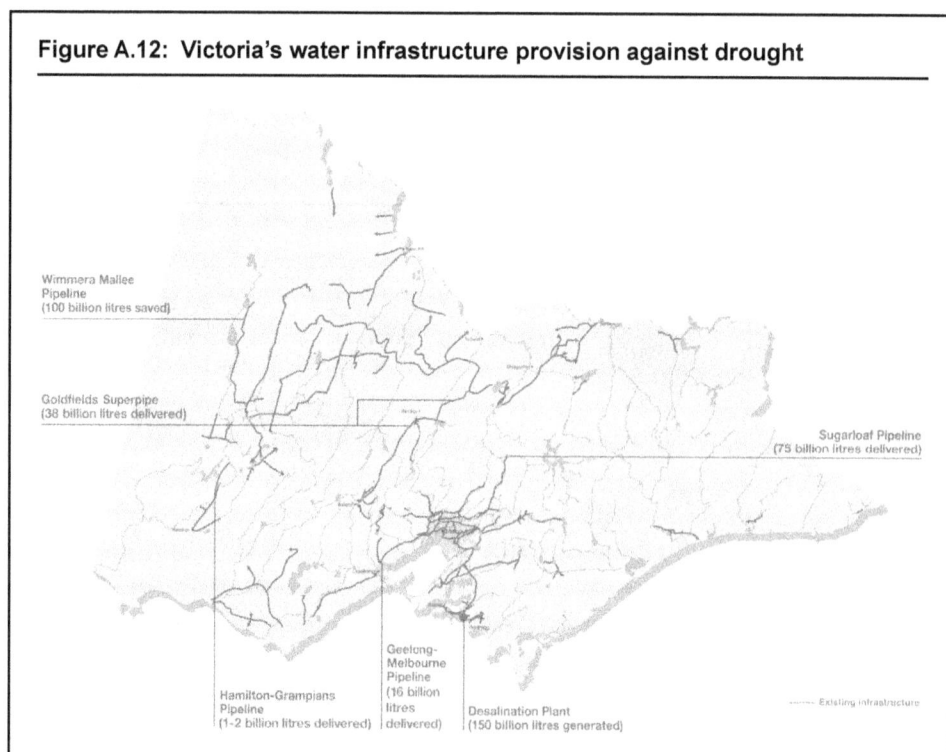

Wimmera Mallee Pipeline
(100 billion litres saved)

Goldfields Superpipe
(38 billion litres delivered)

Sugarloaf Pipeline
(75 billion litres delivered)

Hamilton-Grampians Pipeline
(1-2 billion litres delivered)

Geelong-Melbourne Pipeline
(16 billion litres delivered)

Desalination Plant
(150 billion litres generated)

Existing infrastructure

*Source:* Department of Sustainability and Environment, 2009

## Sustainable Water Strategies (SWS)

The SWS are a critical element in Victoria's strategic approach to securing water resources. Each SWS which covers one of the State's four regional areas must provide strategic planning for the use of water resources as specified in the Water Act.

Each SWS must identify threats in order to improve the reliability of supply and quality of water for both environmental and consumptive uses, and must propose how demand for water will be managed and establish priorities for improving river system environmental health.

The northern Region SWS, completed in November 2009, concerns the major Victorian irrigation areas supplied from the Goulburn and Murray Rivers. The Northern Region SWS identifies threats to water supply over the next 50 years and outlines actions and policies to assist water users, environmental managers and communities manage the consequences of prolonged drought and climate change. The northern SWS recognized:

- The need to protect entitlement security;
- Enhancement of opportunities for irrigators to manage risk;
- The need to increase efficiency for consumptive and environmental water uses; and
- The impact of change on the economy, the environment and the society.

## Application of Modeling to Assess Climate Change Impacts

Modeling assessed the impact of climate change on water resources and reliability of supply to the various entitlement holders, and included, as discussed above, the benefits of reserve rule modification. Figure A.13 shows the impact on river inflows as assessed for four climate change scenarios. The four climate change scenarios were compared to a base case of historic climate extending over a recorded period of 118 years (1890–2007). The climate change scenarios were low, medium and high according to the CSIRO climate change model predictions[10] and an extension of the 1997–2009 drought weather

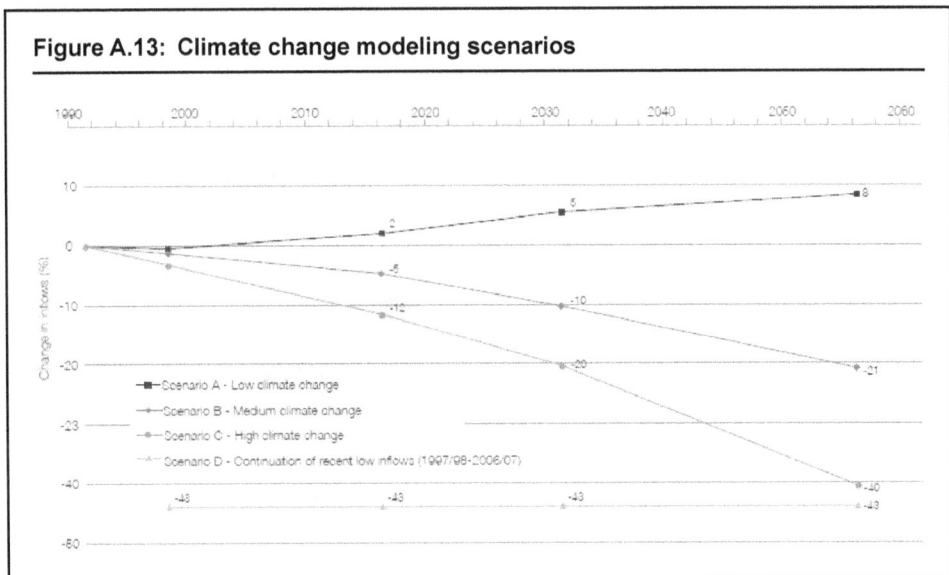

Figure A.13: Climate change modeling scenarios

*Source:* Jones, R. N. and Durack, P. J., 2005

pattern. The simple drought extension scenario has similar impact to the CSIRO high change scenarios over the long term.

## Irrigation Modernization

Investment in irrigation modernization in northern Victoria now totals around $1,500 million and is expected to increase to around $2,500 million. This considerable investment has two main purposes:

- To provide reduced system losses, and distribute water savings to the environment, urban supply and irrigators; and
- To enable major restructuring of the northern irrigation system to ensure sustainability into the future. The restructuring involves both system modernization and reduction of public irrigation systems. The reduction in public assets includes a range of on-farm adjustments from conversion to non-irrigation to significantly improved irrigation efficiency.

The northern Victorian irrigation modernization will reduce system losses and increase water delivery efficiency from the 70 percent to an estimated 85 percent. The total water savings expected from all the irrigation modernizations in northern Victoria will be over 500,000 ML.

Channel automation (to reduce system spillage), introduction of accurate metering (the existing meters under record by almost 10 percent), channel rehabilitation and channel decommissioning will all contribute to water saving. Figure A.14 pictures new infrastructure that is an important part of the irrigation modernization.

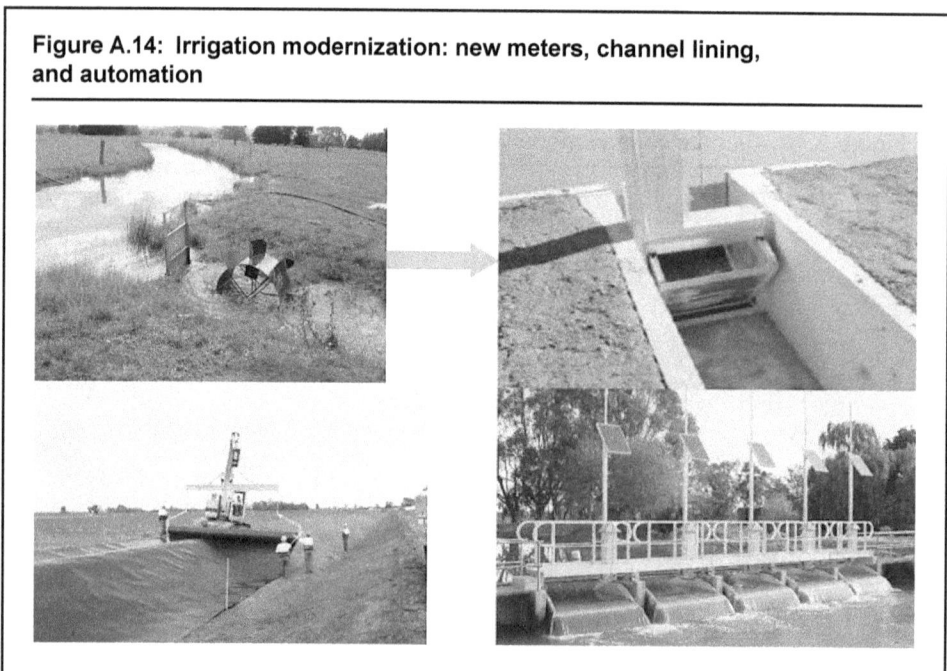

**Figure A.14: Irrigation modernization: new meters, channel lining, and automation**

*Source:* Graeme Turner, 2012

This investment includes a major irrigation sector adjustment component aimed at more efficient on-farm irrigation delivery and a reduction in size of the public owned irrigation system. Irrigation in areas deemed unsuitable is being phased out and delivery capability enhanced in areas deemed most suitable for irrigation. This process of structural change is being undertaken in a cooperative manner which allows some farmers to retire from irrigation and some to increase their irrigating capacity. The net result is to make the irrigation dependent food producing industry of northern Victoria more sustainable.

## Notes

1. See www.ourwater.vic.gov.au/monitoring/monthly/archive.
2. The technical definition of rainfall or runoff variability is the standard deviation divided by the mean for a given time increment.
3. T. A. McMahon et al. 1987. *Runoff variability: a global perspective.*
4. *The Garnaut Climate Change Review*, 2008, identified climate change as a real and growing issue.
5. Index of Stream Condition benchmark surveys are undertaken every five years.
6. Note: a water year is the 12 months starting July 1, while the start of the irrigation season is mid-August (when the deliveries on the channel system commence).
7. Northern Region Sustainable Water Strategy, Department of Sustainability and Environment, Government of Victoria, November 2009.
8. *Securing Our Water Our Future*, State of Victoria, June 2004.
9. Victorian Government, *Our Water Our Future, The Next Stage of the Government's Water Plan*, June 2007
10. Jones, R. N. & Durack, P. J. 2005. *Estimating the Impacts of Climate Change on Victoria's Runoff Using a Hydrological Sensitivity Model*, CSIRO Atmospheric Research, Melbourne, Australia.

# References

Asian Development Bank, World Bank, Japan International Cooperation Agency (2010), Economics of Climate Change Adaptation.

Bates, B. C., Walker, K., Beare, S. & Page, S. 2010. "Incorporating Climate Change in Water Allocation Planning." Waterlines report, National Water Commission, Canberra, Australia.

Blomquist W., Giansante C., Bhat A., Kemper K. 2005. "Institutional and policy analysis of river basin management: The Guadalquivir River Basin, Spain," Policy Research Working Paper 3526, World Bank, Washington DC.

Bureau of Meteorology, Australia (2010), Rainfall patterns and variability of Australia, online climate data.

CSIRO. 2008. "Water Availability in the Murray-Darling Basin. A Report to the Australian Government from the CSIRO Murray-Darling Basin Sustainable Yield Project." Commonwealth Scientific and Industrial Organisation, Australia.

Department of Sustainability and the Environment, 2009. "Northern Region Sustainable Water Strategy, Government of Victoria." http://www.ourwater.vic.gov.au/programs/sws/northern/final, accessed 20 December 2011.

Department of Sustainability and the Environment, 2010. "Goulburn Murray Irrigation District, 2008 Irrigation Modernization Works, Post Implementation Review." Shepparton & Central Goulburn Irrigation Areas, Internal document. Prepared by Department of Sustainability and the Environment, and Matt Ryan Consulting, Melbourne, Australia.

DSEWPC. 2011. "Water in Australia: Water for the Future, Department of Sustainable Environment Water Population Communities." Available at http://www.environment.gov.au/water/australia/index.html, accessed 20 December 2011.

Graeme Turner (2012), Towards Green Water Defense in East Asia: Adaptive Water Scarcity Management under Changing Climate. A study report for the World Bank.

Gunaratnam D. and Li Z. 2010. "Strengthening of water resources management in Guiyang: IWRM towards demand management." Asian Development Bank.

IPCC. 2007. *Climate Change: Impacts, Adaptation and Vulnerability.* Contribution of Working Group II to the Fourth Assessment Report of the Intergovernmental Panel on Climate Change. Parry, M. L., Canziani, O. F., Palutikof, J. P., van der Linden, P. J. and Hansons, C. E. (eds). Cambridge University Press, Cambridge, UK.

Jones, R. N. & Durack, P. J. (2005), Estimating the Impacts of Climate Change on Victoria's Runoff Using a Hydrological Sensitivity Model, CSIRO Atmospheric Research, Melbourne, Australia.

Liu, Y. 2012. *Summary report on the water resources management practices in China.*

Millennium Ecosystem Assessment. 2005. Ecosystems and Human Well-Being: Biodiversity Synthesis. Washington, DC, World Resources Institute.

MARD (2009), US/Israel Binational Agricultural Research and Development Fund—MARD Facilitating Grant Program.

M. Rodell, R. Houborg, B. Li, J. Lawrimore, R. Heim, M. Svoboda, B. Wardlow, B. F. Zaitchik, R. Reichle, J. S. Famiglietti, R. Tinker, and M. Rosencrans (2009), Grace: Monitoring groundwater response to drought, a presentation by NASA GSFC.

National Water Commission. 2010. *The impacts of water trading in the southern Murray-Darling Basin: An economic, social and environmental assessment.* National Water Commission, Canberra, Australia.

National Water Commission. 2011. *National Water Planning Report Card 2011.* National Water Commission, Canberra, Australia.

National Water Commission. 2011b. *The National Water Initiative — securing Australia's water future: 2011 assessment.* National Water Commission, Canberra, Australia.

National Water Commission. 2011c. *National Water Planning Report Card 2011.* National Water Commission, Canberra, Australia.

NTPSWS. 2009. *National Target Program for Sustainable Water Sector.* Vietnam Government Water Sector Review Team. Available at http://www.vnwatersectorreview.com/detail.aspx?pid=107&r=5, accessed 20 December 2011.

OECD. 2010. *OECD review of agricultural policies: Israel.* ISBN: 978-92-64-07939-7.

Ortega Luis, and Fernando Pizarro. (2008), Practical Solutions to Water Challenges: Learning from the Spanish Experience. World Bank–Spain Study Tour 2008. ETWWA, World Bank, Washington, DC.

Peel, M. C., Finlayson, B. L. and McMahon, T. A. 2007. Updated world map of the Koppen-Geiger climate classification. Hydrology and Earth System Sciences, 11, 1633–1644. Available at http://www.hydrol-earth-syst-sci.net/11/1633/2007, accessed 9 January 2012.

Preston, B. L., Suppiah, R., Macadam, I., and Bathols, J. 2006. "Climate Change in the Asia/Pacific Region." A Consultancy Report Prepared for the Climate Change and Development Roundtable, Climate Change Impacts and Risk CSIRO Marine and Atmospheric Research, Commonwealth Scientific and Industrial Research Organization Australia. Available at http://www.csiro.au/files/files/p9xj.pdf, accessed 6 January 2012.

State of Victoria (2004), Securing Our Water Our Future, June 2004.

T. A. McMahon (1987), Runoff variability: a global perspective.

The Israel project (2011), Israeli Innovations in Agrotech Resource Kit.

The Barilla Group, The Coca-Cola Company, The International Finance Corporation, McKinsey & Company, Nestlé S.A., New Holland Agriculture, SABMiller plc, Standard Chartered Bank, and Syngenta AG (2009), Charting our water future: Economic frameworks to inform decision-making.

UK Met Office. 2011. "Climate: Observations, projections and impacts China." Met Office, Devon, United Kingdom, viewed 9 January 2012, http://www.metoffice. gov.uk/media/pdf/4/p/China.pdf accessed 6 January 2012.

Velez, C. E., Yee-Batista, C. and Eiseman, E. H. LCSUW. 2011. *Turning Latin America's water utilities green: lessons from Spain.* The World Bank, Washington, DC.

Victorian Government (2007), Our Water Our Future, The Next Stage of the Government's Water Plan, June 2007.

VROM. 2001. *Het belang van een goede ondergrond.* Ruimtelijke Verkenningen 2000. Den Haag. [in Dutch]

www.tradingeconomics.com/spain.

www.global-warming-forecasts.com/water-supply-shortage-water-scarcity-climate.php www.waterregister.vic.gov.au/

World Bank. 2006. *Water Resources Management in an Arid Environment: The Case of Israel.* Analytical and Advisory Assistance (AAA) Program China: Addressing Water Scarcity Background Paper No. 3., Washington DC.

World Bank. 2007. *Water Conservation Project Implementation Completion Report.* Washington, DC.

World Bank (2008), Asian Mega-City Climate Change Impact Assessment. Washington, DC.

World Bank. 2009. *Addressing China's Water Scarcity: Recommendations for Selected Water Resource Management Issues.* Washington, DC.

World Bank (2010), Climate Change Adaptation in Water Resources Management. Washington, DC.

World Bank. 2010. *Climate Change and Water Resources Management Report, Water Anchor.* Washington, DC.

World Bank. 2011. *World Development Report: Development and Climate Change.* Washington, DC.

World Bank. 2011. "GEF Hai Basin Integrated Water and Environment Management Project Implementation Completion Report" Washington, DC.

## ECO-AUDIT
### *Environmental Benefits Statement*

The World Bank is committed to preserving endangered forests and natural resources. The Office of the Publisher has chosen to print World Bank Studies and Working Papers on recycled paper with 30 percent postconsumer fiber in accordance with the recommended standards for paper usage set by the Green Press Initiative, a non-profit program supporting publishers in using fiber that is not sourced from endangered forests. For more information, visit www.greenpressinitiative.org.

In 2010, the printing of this book on recycled paper saved the following:

- 11 trees*
- 3 million Btu of total energy
- 1,045 lb. of net greenhouse gases
- 5,035 gal. of waste water
- 306 lb. of solid waste

---

* 40 feet in height and 6–8 inches in diameter

green press
INITIATIVE

www.ingramcontent.com/pod-product-compliance
Lightning Source LLC
Chambersburg PA
CBHW080618270326
41928CB00016B/3114